ERRATUM

Through an oversight, the PTE fleets have been omitted from Table 3 on page 112, covering the major UK bus fleets in 1985.

The missing section covering PTE fleets reads:
Passenger Transport Executives and their fleets
Greater Manchester 2,435, Merseyside 1,230, South Yorkshire 1,103, Strathclyde 814, Tyne & Wear 510, West Midlands 2,255, West Yorkshire 1,076.

This in turn affects the list of the ten largest fleets, which should now read:
TEN LARGEST BRITISH FLEETS

London Transport	5,132
Greater Manchester	2,435
West Midlands	2,255
Merseyside	1,230
London Country	1,134
South Yorkshire	1,103
West Yorkshire	1,076
Crosville	933
Ribble	872
Strathclyde	814

BRITISH BUSES
IN COLOUR

BRITISH BUSES
IN COLOUR

Gavin Booth

IAN ALLAN
Publishing

First published 1996

ISBN 0 7110 2477 4

© Ian Allan Ltd 1996

Published by Ian Allan Publishing

an imprint of Ian Allan Ltd, Terminal House, Station Approach, Shepperton, Surrey TW17 8AS
Printed by Ian Allan Printing Ltd, Coombelands House, Coombelands Lane, Addlestone, Surrey KT15 1HY.

Front cover: In the 1950s many operators turned to rebuilding and rebodying wartime buses to prolong their lives. This 1945 Aldershot & District Guy Arab II had received a new 8ft wide East Lancs 56-seat body in 1954 and is seen at Petworth in 1965.
Roger G Funnell

Back cover, top: After classic designs like the RT and Routemaster, London Transport turned to 'off-the-shelf' high-capacity single-deckers in the 1960s, like this AEC Merlin with Strachans 25-seat (plus 48 standing) body at Victoria in 1966 on the first of LT's flat-fare Red Arrow services.
Murdoch Currie

Back cover, bottom: The early Bristol VRTs did not find favour with the Scottish Bus Group which exchanged its examples with FLF type Lodekkas from National Bus Company fleets. Alexander (Midland) set the ball rolling when its 15, with ECW 77-seat bodies, went to Eastern National after a very short time. The example shown at Stirling was new to Midland in March 1970, and had passed to Eastern National by September the following year.
Iain MacGregor

Title page: Two non-standard buses in a fleet that otherwise consisted almost entirely of home-built buses. The giant Midland Red company acquired the Leyland Titan PD2/12 with Leyland body (left) with the business of Kemp & Shaw of Leicester in 1955, and the all-Leyland Royal Tiger PSU1/9 with Leyland bus body (right) from Allen of Mountsorrel.
M Sutcliffe

Half-title page: Daimler and Metro-Cammell are just two of the prominent names of 1950 that have since disappeared from the ranks of British bus manufacturers. This Daimler Fleetline with Alexander-style Metro-Cammell bodywork was new to Bradford City Transport in 1967 and passed to the new West Yorkshire PTE in 1974. It was an early repaint into PTE livery and still carries its Bradford fleetnumber.
H J Black

ACKNOWLEDGEMENTS
The author wishes to thank all the photographers who willingly submitted material for this book. Copies of the photographs credited to 'Photobus' and 'Policy Transport Photos' can be obtained from these organisations: Photobus is at Greenacre Barn House, Howe, Lyth, Cumbria LA8 8DF, and Policy at 15 Scarsdale Avenue, Allestree, Derby DE22 2LA

CONTENTS

Introduction — 5

1 Walkin' back to happiness — 6
The situation in 1950

2 It's now or never — 14
Manufacturers in the 1950s

3 Ticket to ride — 22
Vehicles in the 1950s

4 Tracks of my tears — 40
Trams and trolleybuses

5 Let the heartaches begin — 46
Vehicles in the 1960s

6 We can work it out — 58
The situation in London

7 All or nothing — 66
Manufacturers in the 1960s and 1970s

8 All kinds of everything — 72
The PTEs

9 Seasons in the sun — 80
National Bus Company and Scottish Bus Group

10 Under pressure — 88
Vehicles in the 1970s

11 The winner takes it all — 96
The run-up to deregulation

12 Chain reaction — 100
Manufacturers and vehicles in the 1980s

13 The final countdown — 106
Summing up

Table 1: Major UK bus fleets 1952 — *110*

Table 2: Major UK bus fleets 1968 — *111*

Table 3: Major UK bus fleets 1985 — *112*

INTRODUCTION

THE RESPONSE to colour bus books has paved the way for this first large-format all-colour book dealing with Britain's buses in the postwar period. Colour photography slowly became more popular in the 1950s and 1960s but cost and slow film speeds meant that many bus photographers at this time stuck to black-and-white. Another problem encountered by early colour bus photographers has been deterioration of some types of slide film.

This book uses colour photographs to illustrate the story of Britain's buses between 1950 and 1986. The year 1950 was chosen as the starting-point because it really marked the start of a new era in bus design after manufacturers had recovered from the restrictions of wartime and the pressures of the early postwar years; 1986 heralded the most important changes in the bus industry for more than 50 years, with the introduction of deregulation and the start of the privatisation process, and the buses bought for service in Britain since then have tended to be very different animals from the ones illustrated in this book.

The amazing developments in vehicle layout, size and design over more than three decades are covered, and the book concentrates on buses rather than coaches, and looks particularly at the major operators who tended to buy the vast proportion of new buses and therefore influenced the shape and size of the market and the viability of Britain's ever-shrinking list of bus chassis and body builders.

Where possible I have tried to avoid the pure 'record' shot, particularly those taken in bus stations and garage yards, and have tried to include good-quality photos of buses in service in their natural habitat.

Authors will tell you that finding suitable chapter titles is often the most difficult part of completing a book like this. To capture the mood of the times I have used the titles of pop songs, all but one of which were number one hits.

As editor of the bi-monthly magazine *Classic Bus* I know that there is a great deal of interest in period views of buses in service, and the success of the *'Heyday'* series of colour photo books from Ian Allan Ltd has confirmed this.

For many years Britain led the world in bus design, but during the period covered by this book, manufacturers and operators seemed to lose their way and the domestic manufacturing industry has suffered greatly as a result.

'British Buses in Colour' is a tribute to the British bus industry in its regulated and largely publicly-owned state, and a reminder of makers, operators and liveries no longer to be seen in the very different world of the late 1990s.

Gavin Booth
Edinburgh, 1996

A popular combination in many parts of Britain in the 1960s was the Leyland Leopard with BET-style bodywork, in this case a Yorkshire Traction 1967 Marshall-bodied 53-seater. It has passed to 'Tracky' with the business of County Motors (Lepton) which had previously been jointly owned with fellow BET fleet Yorkshire Woollen, and the then-independent West Riding.
H J Black

IN THE deregulated, privatised 1990s, it is sometimes difficult to remember a time when the British bus industry was highly-regulated, largely publicly-owned, and served by a bewildering array of manufacturers eager to build new buses for operators who were carrying record numbers of passengers. Yet this was certainly the scene in 1950 and while there were ownership changes over the next 35 years, even in 1985 the situation was still one that a 1950s busman would have recognised. After 1985, Conservative free market thinking changed the structure of the industry totally, and the pieces of the jigsaw are still falling into place more than a decade later.

In 1950 the bus industry was beginning to get back on to its feet after a decade of war and austerity. During the 1930s motorbuses had really established a strong position helped by the quality and quantity licensing introduced with the 1930 Road Traffic Act and the great advances in bus design that followed.

London Transport, formed in 1933, was the first of the great conurbation authorities and was leading the way with innovative bus design. The Tilling & BAT group and the British Electric Traction (BET) group were the main forces operating company buses in England and Wales. The Scottish Motor Traction (SMT) group had brought together

Opposite: **Long-lasting survivors were the Portsmouth Corporation Leyland Titan TD4s with the early vee-fronted six-bay style of Leyland metal-framed bodywork. Dating from 1935, some of these buses lasted into the early 1960s.**
A J Douglas/Photobus

Above: **Really old buses could still be found in Jersey in the 1950s, operating for Jersey Motor Transport. This Leyland PLSC3 Lion with 31-seat Leyland body, seen in St Helier, was new in 1929 and long-lived buses like this were eagerly sought by the early bus preservationists. This bus, re-registered JCP 60F, is now in the Science Museum collection.**
G Morant/Photobus

Left: **Another older Leyland that ran through the 1950s is this 1940 Titan TD7 with Leyland bodywork, seen in 1960 when still operating in the then privately-owned West Riding fleet. It had come to West Riding with the 170-bus fleet of J Bullock & Sons in 1950.**
Roger Holmes

the four major Scottish territorial companies, and there were smaller groups like Balfour Beatty and Red & White, as well as significant operators like Barton, Lancashire United and West Riding which were independent of the major groups.

There were about 100 Corporation bus fleets in proud municipal ownership, ranging from mighty Birmingham, Glasgow, Liverpool and Manchester down to tiny Urban District Council fleets like Bedwas & Machen and West Bridgford (see table on page 110). Many still operated trams or trolleybuses, and a few operated both, but the motorbus was on the way up as more and more municipalities abandoned the tramcar, perceived as slow and inflexible in the growing road traffic of the time.

Empty cobbled streets and tramlines typify the 1950s, and fleets like Alexanders were past masters at keeping elderly buses on the road. This 1940 Leyland Tiger TS8 special with 39-seat Alexander body is seen on a Glasgow local service in 1961. Buses like this lasted for up to 24 years in the giant Alexander empire.
G Lumb

Top: **While some fleets quickly sold, rebuilt or rebodied their wartime utility vehicles, others found that they were useful no-frills buses at a time of high passenger demand. This Widnes Corporation Daimler CWA6 has utility Duple lowbridge bodywork.**
G Lumb collection

Above: **The Leyland Titan PD1 was Leyland's first postwar double-deck model, and many were built with this style of Leyland's own bodywork. Warrington Corporation was a good Leyland customer, but in the first postwar decade also bought Bristols and Fodens. Although Warrington bought PD1s like this in 1946, this is an ex-Lytham St Annes 1947 example seen in 1966.**
Michael H C Baker

Then there were the thousands of smaller bus and coach operators, often with just a handful of vehicles running on everything from coach tours and hires to regular market-day services and even intensive urban and inter-urban services. The road service licensing of the 1930 Act had usually protected the incumbent operator against the territorial companies and in many parts of Britain there were pockets of very strong independent operation. The only way the bigger operators could get involved in these often lucrative services was to buy the smaller firms; much of the 1930s expansion by the company fleets was through acquisition.

Continuing austerity

By the time 1950 came the bus industry had coped with the restrictions and shortages of World War 2, and the continuing austerity of the early postwar years. New buses had been severely restricted during the war years, and even after the war the demand for new buses overwhelmed the manufacturers who were being officially urged to concentrate much of their production on export orders to help restore a healthy British economy.

The main trouble was that people wanted to travel. With movement often restricted during the war, there was a pent-up demand for travel and many operators enjoyed their best-ever passenger totals around 1950. Private motoring was still very much for the better-off, and even then cars and petrol were not easy to get. Most people used public transport to and from work, often with an extra journey home at lunchtime, and with television still a very restricted service most people used buses and trams to get to cinemas, theatres and pubs in the evening and at weekends.

The shape of the industry had changed in the early postwar years. The Labour government's nationalisation programme included the mainline railway companies, London Transport and the Tilling and SMT groups, now grouped together under the British Transport Commission (BTC), but the BET group stayed staunchly in private hands. BTC also acquired the Balfour Beatty and Red & White groups and mopped up some other significant independents. There were proposals for area transport boards which could ultimately have covered the whole of Britain, but these were dropped when the Conservatives regained control in 1951.

The other sectors of the industry continued much as before. There were in 1950 some 96 municipal fleets, a number that was to stay fairly steady until the late 1960s. In total over 60% of the 73,000 buses and coaches on the road in 1950 were publicly-owned.

Operators became very adept at keeping the buses of the time on the road. There were many prewar buses still around, a few dating back to the years before the 1930 Act. Buses built from the mid-1930s were still fairly modern in concept with diesel engines and a standard of refinement that some new postwar buses failed to match. To keep the prewar buses going many operators turned to rebuilding and rebodying, which meant that 1930s buses could still be found in many parts of the country in the 1960s.

The restrictions on bus production during the War meant that for most operators only a tiny proportion of the normal annual vehicle intake materialised, and the buses themselves were rugged and utilitarian, a far cry from the

The Bedford OB was popular as a coach chassis in the early postwar years, but was also the mainstay of many fleets in rural areas. This Duple-bodied example in the fleet of Pioneer, Newport, is seen at Goodwick in 1963.
P R Wallis

Leyland's bigger-engined Titan PD2 model was one of the postwar double-deck success stories. This 1948 Exeter Corporation example with Leyland bodywork is seen in company with a 1957 Guy Arab IV/Park Royal from the same fleet and a Devon General AEC Regent V/MCW. The Exeter municipal fleet was one of the first to sell out, to NBC in 1970.
M Sutcliffe

sophisticated vehicles of the late 1930s. Often the chassis of the wartime utility buses were considerably more durable than the bodies which had been built with unseasoned wood and other sub-standard materials, so wartime buses were usually substantially rebuilt, and in many cases rebodied, to give operators reliable and hard-working buses for a fraction of the cost of a new bus.

What new buses there were in the early postwar years would often be little better – and sometimes considerably worse – than their immediate prewar counterparts, but for operators hungry for new stock to replace tired prewar buses and satisfy the apparently insatiable demand for bus travel, anything was welcome.

Bewildering range

There was no shortage of choice. AEC, Albion, Atkinson, Austin, Bedford, Commer, Crossley, Daimler, Dennis,

Foden, Guy, JNSN, Leyland, Maudslay, Morris-Commercial, Seddon, Sentinel and Tilling-Stevens were all anxious to sell chassis, and there was an almost bewildering range of bodybuilders keen to build on these chassis; some were well-established names, others flourished briefly to take advantage of the exceptional demand; only a very few survive to this day.

By 1950 the industry was beginning to settle down again. Deliveries of new vehicles were at last beginning to get through and operators were able to stock their fleets with the buses they really wanted. Vehicle design was changing, partly as a result of prewar experiments and partly because manufacturers had been able to catch their breath and devote time to research and development work.

So the second-generation postwar double-deckers were born, with big understressed engines, following from the work that AEC and Leyland had been doing just before the

War. Models like the AEC Regent III and Leyland Titan PD2 were to set a pattern for the next two decades, and their greatest competition would come from Daimler with its CV range and successive models of Guy Arab. Other manufacturers who dabbled in the double-deck market at the time were Albion, Crossley, Dennis and Foden, but they never matched the sales success of the big four, AEC, Daimler, Guy and Leyland.

Two other significant double-deck manufacturers should not be forgotten. The giant Birmingham & Midland Motor Omnibus Co (BMMO) had a long tradition of building chassis for its Midland Red bus fleet, and would resume its postwar double-deck production with the D5 in 1949. Bristol, again an offshoot of an important operator, had become the principal chassis supplier to the Tilling group, and under BTC control its products were restricted to the nationalised fleets, with bodywork by another operator offshoot, Eastern Coach Works (ECW). Bristol/ECW products became virtually the only type bought by the Tilling group fleets for the next 15 years, and the Scottish Bus Group (SBG), formed from the SMT group, also bought Bristol and ECW products, though it chose to buy on the open market as well. London Transport could have bought Bristol/ECW types but preferred to stick to its normal suppliers except for some small batches of specialised bodies built by ECW.

Full-size single-deck chassis followed a similar pattern. The first postwar models were similar to their prewar

Top: **Red & White was still an independent company until it passed into the Tilling group in 1950 and it was an enthusiastic Albion customer. This 1947 Valkyrie CX13 had received an ECW-style Brislington Body Works body in the early 1950s.**
Arnold Richardson/Photobus

Above: **As a stopgap measure for the Tilling group fleets 100 Leyland PD1A were bought and fitted with ECW bodies, and Crosville was the biggest customer, with 35 of these buses.**
C Nash/Photobus

counterparts, but then more sophisticated big-engined models were introduced by the mainstream manu-facturers and it might have seemed that this was the way things would develop had it not been for flurries of background activity as manufacturers developed a completely new breed of single-decker with a flat engine mounted between the axles under the floor. There had been experimentation with flat engines before the war, and London Transport had bought 88 special Leyland Tigers to this layout in 1937/9, but the war had interrupted development work and it was not AEC or Leyland, who had been heavily involved in this work, who introduced the first of the new postwar breed, but Midland Red with the BMMO S6 in 1946 for its own use and the low-volume Sentinel company in 1948 with the Beadle-Sentinel STC4.

The major manufacturers were not far behind, and by 1950 AEC had introduced the Regal IV, Leyland the Olympic integrally built by Metropolitan-Cammell Weymann (MCW), and there would soon be equivalent chassis from Albion, Atkinson, Bristol, Daimler, Dennis and Guy.

Bedford had carved itself a valuable market niche with its semi-normal control prewar chassis, and its postwar OB model rates as one of the all-time classic designs, usually fitted with a 29-seat Duple Vista coach body and providing operators with a low-cost and reliable small coach for a wide range of work. Although it might have been argued that the OB would still have sold, it was replaced in 1950 by the 'Big Bedford' SB, a forward-control front-engined chassis suitable for coach bodies up to 33 seats, and its main competitor was the Commer Avenger. The SB would dominate this market for many years as the basis of both buses and coaches.

That then was the British bus scene in 1950 when there were over 73,000 buses and 4,700 tramcars in service.

Everything seemed very orderly: competition between bus companies was virtually non-existent under the licensing regime, passenger numbers were booming, new and bigger buses were taking to the roads – everything in the garden seemed to be lovely. ♠

Delivered to Hants & Dorset in 1942, this Bristol K5G had been rebuilt with a lower-mounted radiator and its Brush body had been modernised after the War. It is seen at Reading in 1963 after sale to fellow Tilling company, Thames Valley. *P R Wallis*

The first production underfloor-engined single-deckers were Midland Red's own-build S6s, built in 1946. This shows one of these, as originally built to 27ft 6in x 7ft 6in dimensions, as a 40-seater. They were later lengthened to become 44-seaters.

2 It's now or never
Manufacturers in the 1950s

Foden enjoyed reasonable success in the bus market in the decade after the war. This typically curvaceous lowbridge Massey-bodied 1951 PVD6 model was new to the fleet of Paisley area independent, Smith, Barrhead. Foden was one of the first manufacturers to introduce full-width 'tin fronts'.
Iain MacGregor

OPEN ANY road passenger transport trade paper of the early 1950s and you will find literally pages of advertisements for manufacturers keen to sell their products to operators who were still hungry for new buses and coaches. Companies that had bought regular batches of new vehicles in the 1930s suddenly found the supply drying up in the World War 2 years when only very basic single-deck and double-deck utility buses were available, and then only on an allocation system. Even in the early postwar years it was difficult to get the vehicles they really wanted, and operators found themselves buying unfamiliar chassis and body types just to get new buses.

It was a frustrating time. Passenger numbers peaked in the late 1940s/early 1950s as Britain got back to work and Britons sought to escape the grey austerity years with trips to the seaside and into the country. Bus and coach operators were desperate to provide vehicles to carry them and often found themselves turning to new suppliers, buying secondhand, and indulging in extensive rebuilding and rebodying exercises.

All of which meant that the manufacturers had a field day and they could sell virtually everything they could build, both to home and export customers.

But problems were looming. The postwar travel boom was beginning to run out of steam. Private motoring in the

1930s had been mainly enjoyed by those with money; now models like the Austin A30, Ford Anglia and Morris Minor were tempting many more to abandon public transport for the delights of the private car – a process that has continued relentlessly since that time.

Then there was television. The BBC's television service had opened in 1936, available only in the London area. When television restarted after the war it was still very much a minority interest but once the nationwide network of transmitters brought TV within the grasp of the majority of the population, Britain seemed to be content to sit in front of a TV set rather than venture out in the evenings.

Once bus operators had been able to restock their fleets, many manufacturers found themselves with surplus capacity. Some truck manufacturers who had dabbled in buses decided to stick to trucks. Smaller coachbuilders abandoned the bus business and returned to their mainstream activities. The manufacturing industry adjusted to the 1950s market.

A glance through the advertisement pages of the January 1950 issue of the monthly trade magazine *Bus & Coach* reveals that there are adverts for AEC, BUT, Crossley, Daimler, Foden, Guy, Leyland, Seddon, Sentinel, and Tilling-Stevens – not one of these once-great names are producing bus chassis today.

Above: **AEC's Regent III** with 9.6-litre engine and preselective gearbox was a sophisticated chassis, and proved highly popular throughout Britain. This 1950 example with stylish **Burlingham** 53-seat lowbridge bodywork, one of 20 for the **Scottish Omnibuses** fleet, is seen in Edinburgh bus station in 1963.
R C Ludgate

Left: **Glasgow Corporation** favoured the locally-built **Albion Venturer** until 1953, and one of its last batch, 8ft wide **CX37SW** models, with **Weymann** 56-seat bodywork, is seen in **George Square**.
G Morant/Photobus

The independent Lancashire United fleet was a keen Atkinson customer for a few years, and this is a lightweight **PL745H** model delivered in 1954 with 44-seat Roe bodywork.
Arnold Richardson/Photobus

Trend-setting

AEC, Daimler and Leyland were the giants. AEC's historic links with London Transport meant that this make dominated the streets of the Capital and in 1950 AEC's Southall works in west London was still building the trend-setting RT type Regent chassis, as well as significant numbers of other types for home and export customers. Although a few customers outside London had taken the RT type chassis, the 'provincial' equivalent, the Regent III, was selling well. The single-deck Regal III chassis was still popular but late in 1949 AEC had announced its underfloor-engined Regal MkIV and this would dictate the shape of single-deckers for some years to come.

Dáimler's main customers came from among the municipal operators who found the refined Daimler chassis with its preselector transmission ideal for intense urban work. The postwar CV range offered a choice of Gardner 5LW or 6LW engines, or Daimler's own CD6 unit. The same engine choice was offered in Daimler's single-deck range and many operators chose the CVD6, with Daimler engine, as the basis for luxury coaches.

Like AEC, Leyland had customers across the board, from small independents, municipal operators, company fleets

and London Transport. Its main offerings in 1950 were the double-deck Titan PD2 and single-deck Tiger PS2 chassis but Leyland had teamed up with Metropolitan-Cammell-Weymann to build the underfloor-engined Olympic, first shown in 1949. While the Olympic was an export success, more conservative British operators indicated a desire for a separate chassis on which they could have bodies built to order by their favoured suppliers, and so the Royal Tiger was born.

Outside the big three, but coming up fast, was Guy. For some years Guy had been a relatively small player in the bus market, but a call to build utility double-deck chassis during the war meant that Guys found their way into many fleets throughout Britain and operators liked the reliability and ruggedness of the utility Arab so much that they continued to choose Guys after the war. The main Guy model was the Arab III, usually with Gardner 5LW or 6LW engine.

Missing from the *Bus & Coach* advert pages were Albion, Austin, Bedford, Commer, Dennis, JNSN, Maudslay and Morris Commercial, of whom Bedford was probably the most significant. Bedford's little semi-normal control OB model was still selling well, but later in 1950 it would be replaced by the 'Big Bedford' SB, the first of a long line of full-size forward control models. Dennis, which has enjoyed a phenomenal success in recent years, was not a major force in the 1950s, producing a competent range of models for a small group of faithful customers.

Also missing, for different reasons, were BMMO and Bristol. BMMO, building chassis only for its parent Midland Red fleet, had been building solid, unadventurous bus chassis since 1923 but had experimented in 1935/6 with rear-engined types. These buses were rebuilt with horizontal engines during the war and this experience gave

BMMO a head start after the war. Its first postwar single-deckers, the S6 type, in 1946, were underfloor-engined types, the first to enter production in Britain. BMMO's first postwar double-decker was slower to arrive, but the largely conventional D5 went into production in 1949.

Bristol chassis had long been popular with a wide range of customers, but as an offshoot of the Bristol Tramways operating company its chassis were increasingly favoured by fellow Tilling group companies and often carried Eastern

The Tilling group's standard highbridge bus before the all-purpose Lodekka came along was the KSW model, 27ft long x 8ft wide, with ECW bodywork. This United Auto 1953 example is operating in Carlisle; in 1969 these operations were transferred to Ribble. *Arnold Richardson/Photobus*

Coach Works bodywork, again built by a company within the group. With the nationalisation of the Tilling group Bristol and ECW passed into the control of the new British Transport Commission and the products of the two factories were restricted to state-owned fleets – in essence the Tilling and Scottish groups, London Transport, and the jointly-owned municipal bus fleets in Yorkshire. As we have seen, the Tilling group took virtually nothing else, the Scottish Bus Group took Bristol/ECW as well as generally available vehicles, London Transport took some ECW bodies, and the Sheffield fleet took a handful of ECW bodies. Bristol also built trucks for the state-owned British Road Services fleet.

The January 1950 *Bus & Coach* included adverts for 19 coachbuilders – Beccols, Brockhouse, Bruce, Cravens, Davies, Duple, Dutfield, Heaver, Longwell Green, Mann Egerton, Metropolitan-Cammell-Weymann, Park Royal, Pearsons, Reading, Roberts, Samlesbury, Trans-United, Welsh Metal Industries, Whitson and Yeates; like the chassis-builders who advertised in that issue, not one remains today. Missing from the adverts were Alexander, Beadle, Brush, Burlingham, Crossley, East Lancs, Harkness, Harrington, Leyland, Massey, Northern Coachbuilders, Northern Counties, Plaxton, Roe, Saunders-Roe, Strachans

and Willowbrook; of these, Alexander, East Lancs, Northern Counties and Plaxton survive today.

Rebuilding

These 1950 adverts are worth studying. Park Royal and Welsh Metal Industries feature export vehicles (as do AEC and Leyland among the chassis builders) and Cravens and MCW proudly feature London buses. Salmesbury majored on rebuilding, with a photo of around a dozen Birmingham City Transport Daimler COG5s in its Lancashire coachworks.

While many of these builders could only produce small quantities of custom-built bodies, there was a handful of front-line builders producing substantial numbers. Duple was far and away the leading builder of luxury coach bodies, with Burlingham and Harrington nipping at its heels; Plaxton was not the force it would later become. In terms of

Top: **Birmingham and Manchester built up the biggest postwar fleets of Crossley double-deckers. This Birmingham City Transport DD42 model dates from 1950 and has Crossley 54-seat bodywork to Birmingham design.**
Arnold Richardson/Photobus

Above: **Daimler single-deckers were popular in municipal fleets, often working alongside double-deckers with similar chassis. This Dundee Corporation CVD6 of 1947 with Weymann bodywork is seen later in its life on driver training duties.**
M Sutcliffe

The Leyland-MCW Olympic integral was Leyland's first production underfloor-engined single-decker, and was soon joined by the Royal Tiger, a greater success on the home market. This HR44 Olympic is seen in service with Leyland-based independent J Fishwick & Sons. *M Sutcliffe*

output, MCW and Park Royal were the leaders, best positioned to quote for the sizeable orders coming from the larger fleets. At the next level were East Lancs, Leyland, Massey, Northern Counties and Roe, all building bus bodies, usually double-deckers, for faithful customers, often in the municipal sector.

Then there was Alexander, which had been principally an in-house bodybuilder for the SMT group before the war, but had stayed in private hands when the SMT group was nationalised in 1949. Although the new Scottish Bus Group would continue to be a major customer, Alexander was starting to look for business in other parts of Britain and by the 1960s had become a major force in the industry. By contrast, Eastern Coach Works, as we have seen, passed into state control and its products would only be available to a restricted group of customers until the mid-1960s.

A number of the 1950 coachbuilders would soon disappear or give up building bus bodies. By the end of the decade the principal survivors would be Alexander, Beadle, Burlingham, Duple, East Lancs, Harrington, Massey, MCW,

Northern Counties, Park Royal, Plaxton, Roe and Willowbrook.

In 1950 the major manufacturers seemed virtually impregnable. Nobody would have dared to prophesy that AEC, Bristol, Daimler and Leyland – or Duple, ECW, MCW and Park Royal – would be mere memories less than 50 years later, and that a substantial proportion of the new buses entering service would be built by Dennis, or by Swedish-owned companies. In the innocent days of the 1950s there was no suggestion that British operators would ever have to turn to European makers for chassis. Indeed at that time Britain was supplying many parts of the world with buses and there was no reason to think that this situation would ever change. ♠

Top: **Seddon has been active as a builder of bus chassis at various times since the war. This rare Seddon Pennine Mk10 with Duple 44-seat body was supplied to West Riding in 1954.**
M Sutcliffe

Above: **Ribble, a committed Leyland customer, was caused some consternation – not least at Leyland – when it bought Sentinels in 1949/51. This is one of its 1951 batch of 44-seat STC6 models.**
D Kerrison/Photobus

The standard Bristol/ECW underfloor-engined offering for state-owned fleets was the Bristol LS with ECW bodywork. This 1955 LS5G of Wilts & Dorset is seen in Winchester in 1963.
P R Wallis

I F THE first postwar buses seemed little different from their prewar brothers, by 1950 the manufacturers were ready to change all that. Exciting development work carried out in the 1930s had seen AEC develop the side-engined Q model, and the trend-setting RT type Regent, and immediately before the war had built an underfloor-engined prototype for Canada. Leyland had built under-floor-engined and rear-engined buses in small quantities for London Transport. Now that the immediate pressures of the postwar years had eased, the designers could get back to the business of refining and developing the bus.

The trend towards bigger engines that had started in the 1930s was continued with the general introduction of the AEC 9.6-litre, the Albion 9.9-litre, the 8.15-litre Bristol AVW, the 8.6-litre CD6 and 10.5-litre CD650 from Daimler, the 10.35-litre Meadows 6DC630, and the 9.8-litre Leyland O.600. The popular and fuel-efficient 7.0-litre Gardner 5LW and 8.4-litre 6LW engines continued to be specified by many operators, with many taking the 6LW, where in prewar days, the 5LW would have been chosen.

AEC and Leyland had proved that a big engine working at less than its full power output was more efficient than a

smaller engine, and anyway buses were getting bigger and heavier and the extra power was often needed.

For urban work many of the larger fleets had chosen chassis fitted with preselector gearboxes, to ease the driver's task; Daimler had standardised on preselectors in the mid-1930s, and AEC offered them on its MkIII versions of its Regal single-deck and Regent double-deck models. Other builders fitted preselectors to special order, but normally offered more basic, usually constant mesh, gearboxes; Leyland offered a synchromesh box on its PD2 and PS2 models.

Changes in vehicle length and width legislation have tended to encourage interest in new types. Full-size buses in 1945 could be up to 7ft 6in wide and 26ft (double-deckers) or 27ft 6in (single-deckers) long. From 1946 8ft wide buses were allowed, initially on approved routes, and by 1950 double-deckers could be 27ft long.

The underfloor-engined single-decker really took off after the June 1950 relaxation which permitted 30ft x 8ft single-deckers. The first underfloor single-deckers to the old 27ft 6in length were typically 40-seaters but the length increase allowed bodybuilders to fit 44 or 45 seats in a saloon lacking

Leyland offered its own body-work for the heavyweight Royal Tiger underfloor-engined chassis, to a rather more severe style than some of its contemporaries. Isle of Man Road Services operated this example, seen in Douglas.
Policy Transport Photos

AEC's equivalent heavyweight model was the Regal IV, and this short (27ft 6in) Park Royal-bodied bus had been an AEC demonstrator before sale to Douglas Corporation.
Policy Transport Photos

A late-model home-market Leyland Tiger, a PS2/1 with East Lancs 35-seat rear-entrance body of the Rawtenstall Corporation fleet.
A Moyes

Western Welsh built up a substantial fleet of Leyland's lighter-weight Tiger Cub model. This 1954 example, like many others in the fleet, has 44-seat Weymann bodywork. The conductor prepares to alight in this 1963 Bridgend scene.
P R Wallis

any engine intrusion and for the first time high-capacity single-deckers came closer to double-deck capacities. For a highbridge double-decker, 56 was the near-universal seating capacity; lowbridge double-deckers with side gangways upstairs typically had seats for 53 or 55.

Midland Red placed the first modern-style underfloor engined single-deckers, with entrances ahead of the front axle, in service in 1946; these were its own-make BMMO S6 model. Though other manufacturers were not far behind, these were not from among the mainstream builders. Beadle, which had already won substantial business from operators with its rebuilds using older components in an integrally-constructed body, linked with steam vehicle manufacturer, Sentinel, to offer the first production underfloor-engined bus. This appeared at the 1948 Commercial Motor Show, the first after the war, and though it sold in small numbers and even won business from Ribble, its main claim to fame is that it was the first on the market.

AEC and Leyland were not far behind. Leyland also went along the integral route, and launched the Olympic, produced with bodybuilder MCW, in 1949. The same year AEC introduced the Regal IV chassis. These models featured horizontal versions of the Leyland O.600 and AEC 9.6-litre engines.

In 1950, the same year 30ft single-deckers on two axles were legalised, the rush was on to produce underfloor-engined chassis. Guy introduced the Arab UF and Atkinson, a new name on the bus market, the PM746H; these both featured horizontal versions of Gardner's popular LW range. Bristol also used horizontal Gardner

engines in its semi-integral LS model, and added a horizontal version of its own AVW engine. Dennis launched the Dominant using its own O6 engine, but this chassis never went into production. Leyland realised that UK operators were not really ready for integral construction and introduced the Royal Tiger, mechanically similar to the Olympic, but a separate chassis; the Olympic carried on to be one of Leyland's most successful export models.

The floodgates were open and the industry very quickly embraced the new underfloor models; the full-sized front-engined single-decker went out of fashion virtually overnight. Daimler's slightly late entry to this market in 1951 was the Freeline with a choice of Gardner 6HLW or Daimler CD650 engines. Dennis ditched the Dominant in favour of the simpler Lancet UF in 1952. Bristol replaced its semi-integral LS model with the MW chassis in 1957.

Revised ranges

But just as the first generation of underfloor-engined chassis were getting established the manufacturers were working on revised ranges. Rising fuel costs and the start of the decline in passenger numbers meant that operators were becoming concerned about cost-saving. A new breed of lighter underfloor chassis with smaller engines was rushed out and most operators turned away from the heavyweights; the new models carried as many passengers but could be around two tons lighter, and while they may have lacked power they were considerably cheaper to run.

Leyland's new model was the Tiger Cub with a new engine, the 5.76-litre O.350. This appeared in 1952, and the same year Guy introduced its Arab LUF. The next year

West Riding bought several batches of AEC's medium-weight Reliance. Its second batch, bought in 1956, had 44-seat Roe bodywork, and one is seen at Wakefield bus station in 1968.
H J Black

AEC responded with the Reliance and Monocoach. These were closely related: the Reliance was a chassis and the Monocoach was intended for integral construction. They offered a choice of engines, the 6.75-litre AH410 and the 7.58-litre AH470, though the AH470 was much more popular. Atkinson introduced lightweight versions of its underfloor models in 1953.

Several operators saw the underfloor-engine layout as an opportunity to introduce buses with a smaller seating capacity but a substantial amount of space for standing passengers. The attraction for traffic staff was that single-deckers could carry as many passengers as double-deckers, but while these buses were briefly fashionable, British passengers soon made it clear that they preferred a seat, and most of these experiments fizzled out.

Not every chassis maker chose to follow the same route. Foden, enjoying a brief spell building buses as well as its more familiar trucks, introduced a rear-engined single-deck chassis, the PVR, in 1950; this was the first commercially available rear-engined chassis to be offered on the UK market, but just over 50 were sold before production ceased in 1954.

The development of the double-deck bus was rather less dramatic in the early 1950s, although they were looking rather different as operators specified full-width fronts in

place of the usual exposed radiators. Foden had started things off with its PVD range in 1945 and then came the BMMO D5 for Midland Red in 1949. Birmingham City Transport, perhaps noting the modern look of Midland Red's buses on the city streets, designed a style that was fitted to Crossleys, Daimlers and Guys for its fleet from 1950. The Birmingham front was adopted by Daimler and Guy for other customers, though exposed radiators continued to be available, and later Dennis used a variation for its Lance K4.

Midland Red bought 100 Leyland Titans in 1952 and specified a full-width front; this front was available as an option on the mainstream Titan range from the following year. AEC fitted some Regent chassis with Birmingham-style fronts but developed its own distinctive design, based on the AEC radiator, for the new Regent V model introduced in 1954.

Bristol's Lodekka had first been shown with a broader version of the normal Bristol radiator but when production started in 1953 a new full-width front was standard.

The double-deckers of the early 1950s had reached a high level of refinement, front-engined chassis with big engines and better gearboxes, but there were far-reaching changes round the corner. AEC's success with underfloor-engined single-deckers prompted it to explore the possibility of an underfloor-engined double-decker. One was built, designated Regent IV, but the inevitably high floor line was a problem and it seemed to offer no real advantages over its more conventional brethren.

Rear engines

Leyland ploughed a different furrow. It had long been interested in rear engines and could look to experience in the United States where rear-engined transit buses were fast becoming standard in the late 1930s. A prototype double-decker, the Lowloader, emerged from Leyland in 1952, an exercise to test operator reaction to this layout. In terms of body layout the Lowloader owed much to conventional thinking on double-deckers. It had a rear entrance, and the front axle was right at the front, under the driver. But the rear platform was shared with the engine, a turbocharged version of the new O.350 engine fitted to the Tiger Cub, chosen no doubt because of its compact proportions; it was coupled to a Wilson preselector gearbox.

The Lowloader was tested by major fleets and a second bus was built in 1954, but by that time Leyland's thinking had changed and the designers were now looking forward to a change in length regulations which would allow a more practical rear-engined double-decker to be designed. That change came in June 1956 when 30ft long double-deckers were authorised and just three months later Leyland astonished the bus industry with the prototype Atlantean, a bus that would set the double-deck trend for the next 40 years.

The Atlantean had the big Leyland O.600 engine mounted transversely behind the rear axle and had a setback front axle with the door alongside the driver. Leyland's preoccupation with integral construction meant that the Atlantean prototype was developed jointly with MCW as a semi-integral lowheight bus, but customers were suspicious and preferred the idea of a separate chassis on which they could have bodies built to their specification by their favoured bodybuilders. So when the Atlantean was finally launched as a production vehicle in 1956 it was revealed as a separate chassis, which meant that the lowheight capability had to be sacrificed. For many

Top: **Many operators stuck to exposed radiators in preference to 'modern' tin-fronts. A Maidstone & District Leyland Titan PD2/12 of 1954 carries an early example of the ultra-lightweight MCW Orion style of bodywork. The unequal-depth windows on the Orion are less obvious on a bus in this traditional livery.**
Roy Marshall/Photobus

Above: **Another operator to choose exposed radiators was East Yorkshire. This 1956 AEC Regent V carries Willowbrook 56-seat bodywork complete with distinctively-shaped Beverley Bar upper deck profile to pass through the Gothic arch in that town. In the background is a Hull Corporation Atlantean.**
P Eckersley/Photobus

Uniquely in the Tilling group Brighton Hove & District carried this non-standard red/cream livery, and this 1952 Bristol KSW6B with ECW 60-seat body at Old Steine in 1962 was typical of the double-deckers it bought right through to 1956.
Iain MacGregor

When Midland Red went to Leyland for 100 Leyland-bodied Titan PD2/12s in 1952/3 it worked with Leyland to develop a full-width bonnet design that would fit in with its own-make double-deckers. The resulting style was adopted by Leyland as its standard in 1953, although the combination of this body style and front end was not supplied new to any other operators, and Leyland closed its bodybuilding department in 1954.
G Morant/Photobus

Foden won a late order for its PVD6 chassis when Warrington Corporation bought five with 58-seat East Lancs bodies in 1956. One is seen in 1970.
Iain MacGregor

operators in urban areas this was not a problem as their fleets were generally of normal-height (approx 14ft 6in) buses. For operators with low bridge (and sometimes low garage roof) problems, Leyland offered a rather awkward compromise – a lowheight (13ft 4in) body that had normal seating on the forward part of the upper deck but a nearside side gangway and four rows of four-across seats at the rear.

Revolutionary as the Atlantean undoubtedly was, many of the most conservative operators continued to buy conventional designs for the front-engined double-decker was far from dead. Indeed other new 1950s designs pushed the barriers back. The most advanced design was the AEC Routemaster, developed for London Transport and described in detail in chapter 6, but there were exciting new models for customers outside London.

AEC's main double-deck offering from 1954 was the Regent V, a lighter-weight chassis typically with a full-width front offering the choice of the 7.68-litre AV470 or 9.6-litre AV590 engines coupled to synchromesh or direct selection epicyclic gearboxes. From 1956 the Regent V was available to 30ft length. But AEC was also looking at the lowheight market, so successfully catered for in the nationalised fleets by the Bristol Lodekka. The Bridgemaster was introduced in 1956, a conventional front-engined bus but integrally

constructed with a Park Royal body. As other builders found, the market for lowheight buses was small and only 180 were built in seven years.

BMMO's main double-deck model in the 1950s was the D7 and 350 were built between 1953 and 1958. These had lightweight bodies by MCW. The D7 was replaced by the D9, an altogether more advanced model, 30ft long with independent front suspension, power steering, servo-assisted disc brakes, and integrally constructed. The D5 and D7 models had been fitted with BMMO's own 8.0-litre engine, but the D9 got a more powerful 10.5-litre engine.

Bristol was still producing longer and wider versions of its K chassis alongside the Lodekka and the last examples entered service in 1957. Over 2,000 of the original LD-series Lodekka were built between 1953 and 1959, with a choice of Gardner 5LW or 6LW or Bristol AVW engines. The next generation of Lodekka was the F-series, with a flat lower saloon floor and air suspension on the rear. These went into production in 1959 and over 3,000 were built; the most popular model was the FLF, 30ft long with a forward entrance.

Dennis also dabbled in the lowheight market, and made an agreement with Bristol to build the Lodekka under licence as the Loline. This chassis was available with Gardner 6LW or 6LX, AEC AV470 or Leyland O.600 engines. The Gardner 6LX engine, introduced in 1958, was a more powerful (10.45-litre) option to the 6LW and was soon the standard choice for most operators.

Guy's main 1950s double-decker was the Arab IV, an improved version of the sturdy wartime and early postwar chassis, based largely on a specification produced by Birmingham City Transport for a batch of 300. From 1956 a 30ft Arab IV was available. Gardner 5LW, 6LW and 6LX engines were offered, as was the Meadows 6DC.

Advanced chassis

But Guy was looking ahead and in 1959 launched the Wulfrunian, an advanced chassis that combined a front engine (the Gardner 6LX) with an entrance ahead of the front wheels, and such features as independent front suspension and disc brakes. Developed largely for the West Riding company, the Wulfrunian was not a success and only 137 were built.

Leyland's Titan PD2 continued to be available right through the 1950s, with a growing range of options – exposed radiator or 'tin front', air or vacuum brakes, synchromesh or epicyclic gearbox. It was joined by the 30ft long PD3 in 1956.

Light weight and high capacity characterise the 1950s. The decade started with double-deckers weighing up to eight tons and seating 56 passengers, and ended up with similarly-sized buses weighing less than seven tons and carrying up to ten passengers more. The longer 30ft double-deckers could usually seat up to 72 and Atlanteans had seats for 78.

The full-size buses of the time, 30ft long by 8ft wide, seem small compared with the buses of today and it is sobering to

After experience with Guy Arabs during the war, many operators continued to buy this chassis. East Kent built up a fleet of MkIV Arabs with Park Royal bodywork between 1952 and 1957, though this bus, the 1952 prototype, had bodywork built by Guy. The similarity of the body to the classic London Transport RT type is evident.
A J Douglas/Photobus

realise that today's midibuses, often 9.8/9.9-metres long, are almost 10% longer than the full-size buses of the 1950s.

There was little interest in shorter buses at the time; operators were constantly pressing for length and width regulations to be relaxed and as we shall see there were some more significant increases in dimensions to come in the next decade. Bedford and Commer, soon to be joined by Ford, catered for operators looking for cheaper, lighter chassis – mainly for coaching work but many smaller operators chose chassis of this type for rural bus work.

Albion saw a niche for a short-length (up to 24ft) underfloor-engined chassis, the Nimbus, from 1955; other builders stuck to front-mounted engines. Bristol's solution to the rural bus problem was the SC, a simple design with a Gardner 3.8-litre 4LK engine, and built nearly 300 for Tilling group companies between 1955 and 1961. Dennis went for the normal control layout with the driver behind the engine for the 4LK-engined Falcon of 1954-6, as did Guy for the Perkins P6-engined NLLVP, essentially a variation on its Vixen chassis to suit London Transport.

The bus bodybuilders had their part to play in the

changing shape and weight of 1950s vehicles. The lead given by designs like the body for London's RT type double-deckers encouraged other builders to go for cleaner, smoother lines, and the new single-deck underfloor-engined chassis gave bodybuilders much more scope to design modern-looking bodies.

The first double-deck bodies after the war were very similar to their prewar counterparts, but as the bus business stabilised after the postwar boom thought was given to cleaner designs more in keeping with the modern image the bus industry was trying to promote.

The move to full-width fronts gave double-deckers a more modern look, though it can be argued that not all of the designs sat comfortably with their bodywork. The neatest

combinations were often those that had been designed as a whole – the BMMO D5, the Bristol Lodekka and the AEC Routemaster are good examples.

Attractive bodies

Some particularly attractive double-deck bodies were around in the early 1950s: Leyland, Park Royal and Roe built some very elegant designs, for example. Improved glazing methods were giving bodies a smoother and more rounded look and many builders went for the sleeker four-bay window layout (introduced in the 1930s by Roe and featured on the RT family) in place of the more common five-bay layout.

South Wales Transport was an enthusiastic AEC user and bought large batches of Regent V in the 1950s and 1960s. This 1956 example seen in Llanelly in 1963 has 56-seat Orion-style Weymann lowbridge bodywork.
P R Wallis

Newly-independent Alexander was beginning to develop its own four-bay designs in place of the Leyland-derived designs it had previously used and while at this time its customers were largely the Scottish Bus Group and Scottish municipal companies, it was beginning to win orders from other parts of Britain.

Burlingham, best known for its luxury coach bodies, offered an attractive and distinctive double-deck design with heavily-radiused window corners and this appeared both on new chassis and on rebodied older chassis.

Duple, the principal coach bodybuilder, had built a stylish four-bay double-deck body for various customers, notably the Red & White group, and in 1952/3 built 60 lightweight bodies on secondhand London Transport Guy Arab chassis for Edinburgh Corporation. As time went on Duple concentrated more and more on single-deckers.

ECW bodies, now almost exclusively on Bristol chassis, were to an instantly recognisable style that had evolved since the early postwar period. The body style developed for the Lodekka was a classic, dealing sympathetically with the inevitable clash between a high driving position and a low-built lower saloon.

The two Wigan-based double-deck builders, Massey and Northern Counties, would eventually merge, but in the 1950s they were building their own distinctive designs, often for municipal customers.

MCW had two distinct arms, the Metropolitan-Cammell Carriage & Wagon Co (MCCW) factory near Birmingham and the Weymann factory at Addlestone. Although there was in theory a range of standard designs which could have

For much of the 1950s Midland Red's standard double-decker was the BMMO D7 with Metro-Cammell bodywork. A total of 350 were built between 1953 and 1958; this bus, seen in the company of Coventry Corporation Daimlers, dates from 1957.
Arnold Richardson/Photobus

Aberdeen Corporation favoured AECs and Daimlers, and here a Daimler CVG6 (left) and an AEC Regent V sit side by side in Union Street in 1971. Both have MCW Orion bodies, the Daimler dating from 1957 and the AEC from 1958. They represent high-capacity 27ft double-deckers; the Daimler has seats for 64, the AEC for 66.
Iain MacGregor

been built at both factories, in practice MCCW built the mainstream higher-volume bodies and Weymann built the more specialised designs – often the single-deckers, the lowheight double-deckers, etc.

MCW had pioneered all-metal bodies in the 1930s and 20 years later were leading the field in ultra-lightweight double-deck bodies. The infamous Orion body, first introduced in 1952, could reduce body weight down to 2ton 5cwt, and complete buses could weigh in at little more than 6.5tons – up to 1.5 tons lighter than equivalent buses from other builders. This inevitably involved some sacrifices; out

went fancy wood finishes and double-skin domes, even interior panels, but operators seeking fuel economy through weight-saving were delighted. The design of the Orion broke away from the norm with its deep lower-deck windows and shallower upper-deck windows, but while the purists were unhappy, this would be a 'look' that would feature on double-deckers for a number of years.

Park Royal and Roe, together as part of the Associated Commercial Vehicles (ACV) group since 1949 (with AEC, Crossley and Maudslay) built both to common designs and to their own distinctive designs. Park Royal's main double-

deck body of the early 1950s owed much to the RT, while Roe's best-remembered designs were the deep-windowed bodies evolved from 1930s prototypes. Crossley also built double-deck bodies through the 1950s.

Willowbrook's metal double-deck bodies were notable for their thick upper-deck front corner pillars, particularly on the special 30ft Sunbeam trolleybuses built under special dispensation from 1954 – two years ahead of the general length relaxation.

The bodywork for the Leyland Atlantean was first developed with MCW and then Alexander and soon most of the main builders had developed fairly uninspired body

designs for this totally new shape of bus. It would be the 1960s, often following pressure from operators, before more stylish designs were introduced.

Most builders were moving to all-metal construction in the 1950s, some using steel, an increasing number using lighter aluminium alloy, some using both. Others, notably Roe, stuck to composite construction, using teak, steel and aluminium.

Coachbuilders certainly went to town with luxury coach bodies on the new single-deck underfloor-engined chassis, but tended to be more conservative with bus bodies on

Above: **Possibly the most famous of the 30ft forward-entrance double-deckers were the Southdown 'Queen Marys', Leyland Titan PD3s with Northern Counties fully-fronted bodies. 285 were built between 1957 and 1967; this is a 1960 example in the traditional and much-loved Southdown livery.**
Roy Marshall/Photobus

Left: **Typical of many early Leyland Atlanteans with MCW bodywork, this Weymann-built PDR1/1 was new in 1962 to the Sheffield Corporation C fleet, but had passed to Yorkshire Woollen when photographed in Dewsbury in 1971.**
H J Black

similar chassis, which were often disappointingly box-like. Given the need to accommodate 44 or 45 passengers within the dimensions this may have been inevitable, but some builders did manage to achieve stylish designs.

The volume builders of single-deck bus bodies in the 1950s were Alexander, ECW, MCW and Park Royal, with smaller quantities from the builders who normally concentrated on coaches, like Burlingham, Duple, Harrington and Plaxton, or those who normally built double-deck bodies, like East Lancs, Massey, Northern Counties and Roe.

One of the most distinctive single-deck bus bodies of the time was built on Leyland Tiger Cub chassis by Saro (Saunders-Roe), which blossomed briefly as a bus bodybuilder in the 1940s and 1950s building RTs for London Transport and substantial export orders, for example.

There were casualties among the bodybuilders in the 1950s, notably Brush, Crossley, Leyland and Saro, as well as a long list of the smaller builders that had emerged after the war. Brush, once one of the country's most important builders, sold its bus business to Willowbrook in 1952 and six years later Willowbrook sold out to Duple. Leyland, which had built bodies right from its earliest days only on its

Left: **The BET fleet James of Ammanford had one of the very first Leyland Atlanteans, and had bought 13 by the time the company was absorbed into South Wales Transport in 1962. This 1960 example, seen running with South Wales in 1963, is of the semi-lowbridge type, with Weymann 73-seat body.** P R Wallis

Above: **Maidstone & District was another early Atlantean customer. This 1959 example has Metro-Cammell 78-seat bodywork.**
Roy Marshall/Photobus

Right: **Guy's answer to the Atlantean, developed for West Riding, was the front-engined Wulfrunian, but the advanced technical specification and the poor roads in that part of Yorkshire caused great problems, and the buses were withdrawn prematurely.** Arnold Richardson/Photobus

own chassis, closed its bodybuilding department in 1954; always keen to work closely with bodybuilders to produce a complete vehicle, Leyland had already linked with MCW to produce the Olympic, and did the same with the Atlantean, but this link would be broken in the 1960s when take-overs brought other coachbuilders into the Leyland empire. ♠

Bradford Corporation's trolleybus system was the last in Britain, closing in 1972. In the final years its main vehicles were rebodied secondhand buses, like this former Darlington 1949 BUT 9611T with 1962 East Lancs 66-seat body, seen in 1962.
Roger Holmes

ELECTRICITY had played a significant part in urban public transport since the turn of the 20th century. Municipal and company electricity generation meant that electric trams and trolleybuses were an economical alternative to petrol-engined and later diesel-engined motorbuses.

But the world was changing. The nationalisation of electricity in 1948 took away local control, and the growing problem of congestion as more private cars took to the roads was causing many towns and cities to reconsider their public transport needs. As more and more local authority housing was built operators were recognising that route extensions and diversions were costly when trackwork and overhead wiring were taken into account, and trams were considerably more expensive to buy new than the more flexible motorbus. Trams had the advantage of much longer lives, but in many towns much-rebuilt 1920s trams could not compare well with 1950s motorbuses.

The move away from tramcars had begun long before World War 2. In the 1920s there had been some 14,000 trams in the UK; by 1945 that total had dropped to 6,200, and after the once-massive Glasgow system closed in 1962 there were fewer than 200.

They succumbed to the all-conquering bus – usually motorbuses, but trolleybuses continued to replace trams in some towns. They succumbed, but not without a fight, it must be said, and there were some very acrimonious confrontations as local residents resisted the proposals of Corporation managers. The British tramcar was typically a double-decker, using tracks mounted in the centre of the road. Some of the more forward-looking undertakings had built reserved track in the suburbs, but most passengers needed to brave the traffic to board and alight from trams.

Some very fine trams were still taking to the roads in the postwar years as systems like Aberdeen (to 1949), Edinburgh (to 1950), Sheffield (to 1952), Blackpool and Leeds (to 1953) and Glasgow (to 1954) continued to replace older cars, but most of these would be scrapped after less than a decade in service – sometimes much less.

The continental approach where tramways were seen as a positive advantage in congested urban centres and given segregated tracks and other priorities, was not followed and only in recent years have we seen the introduction of modern tramways in Britain, in Manchester and Sheffield.

Healthier

The trolleybus was in an altogether healthier state, with 38 systems still surviving in 1950. The majority were municipal systems, though the Tilling companies Brighton Hove & District and Notts & Derby had trolleybuses, as did British Electric Traction's Hastings and Mexborough & Swinton companies; the Llanelli trolleybuses were briefly in the control of the South Wales Electricity Board as a consequence of nationalisation, and South Lancashire

South Lancashire Transport, associated with the Lancashire United Transport motorbus company, operated trolleybuses until 1958. This elderly-looking Leyland TTB4 with Roe 64-seat body, was new in 1936 and lasted until 1956.
G Morant/Photobus

Transport was independently owned. Then of course there was the giant London Transport system.

Twenty-five trolleybus systems survived after 1960, but the 1960s saw some significant casualties including Belfast (1968), Bournemouth (1969), Glasgow (1967), Huddersfield (1968), Hull (1964), London (1962), Manchester (1966), Newcastle (1966), Nottingham (1966), Portsmouth (1963) and Wolverhampton (1967), all of which had fleets of more than 100 trolleybuses – some considerably more. In 1950 London had some 1,800, and Belfast and Newcastle each had over 200.

Large quantities of new trolleybuses were placed in service after the war, though the pace was slowing down by the 1960s. One system, Glasgow, had not actually started operating trolleybuses until 1949 and placed its last new vehicles in service in 1958; the system closed in 1967. Other operators buying trolleybuses in the 1960s were Bournemouth and Reading, but these fine vehicles often saw very little service; although the Bournemouth Sunbeams ran for only seven years, five of a batch of 12 Reading Sunbeams went on after seven years service there to run for Teesside for another two or three years.

Other operators had older trolleybuses rebodied, including Bradford, Doncaster, Rotherham, Teesside and Wolverhampton, and some systems snapped up the bargains that came on to the secondhand market when others closed. Bournemouth, Bradford, Maidstone, Teesside and Walsall kept their fleets topped-up in this way.

Although there had been a wide range of trolleybus builders before the war the numbers dwindled quickly in the postwar period. Crossley, Daimler, Guy and Ransomes all built trolleybuses at this time, but after 1951 only two builders were left. British Electric Traction (BUT) took over the trolleybus-building activities of AEC and Leyland in 1946, and over the years various AEC-designed double-deckers were built at factories at Kingston, Southall and Stockport, while Leyland concentrated on single-deck models at its Kingston, Leyland and Watford plants.

The BUT double-deck model range for the UK market comprised the 9611T, 9612T, 9613T and 9641T chassis. The first three were two-axle models, respectively for 26ft, 27ft and 30ft bodywork, while the 9641T was a three-axle 30ft chassis. Single-deck BUT chassis were rarer in the UK: Glasgow Corporation bought RETB1 models in 1951/3 and 1958, the newer buses being 35ft buses operated on a special dispensation three years before the length regulations were relaxed from 30ft to 36ft.

In 1948 Guy Motors bought the Sunbeam Trolleybus Co, and its main trolleybus models were the F4 and F4A, S7 and S7A, and MF2B. The F4/F4A were two-axle chassis, the S7/S7A were three-axle chassis, and the MF2B was a two-axle chassis with a setback front axle. A Walsall F4A was the first 30ft two-axle bus for a UK customer when the Corporation got special permission in 1954 to run a batch of 22, two years ahead of the universal 30ft length limit. A Bournemouth MF2B, delivered in October 1962, was the last trolleybus delivered to a British operator unless you

Top: **A fine 1951 BUT 9641T with 70-seat Brush bodywork in the Nottingham Corporation fleet. The Nottingham system closed in 1966.**
D Kerrison/Photobus

Above: **Maidstone Corporation operated a batch of 12 1946 Sunbeam W with Northern Coachbuilders 56-seat bodies. The Maidstone trolleybus system closed in 1967.**
A J Douglas/Photobus

Reading operated some impressive three-axle trolleybuses like this 1950 Sunbeam S7 with 69-seat Park Royal bodywork, fitted with platform doors, unusual for an urban bus of this time. The Reading trolleybus system closed in 1968.
P R Wallis

Glasgow Corporation opened its trolleybus system in 1949 and its last new vehicles were 1957/8 **BUT 9613T** with attractive Crossley 71-seat bodies. The Glasgow trolleybus system only lasted until 1967.
Gavin Booth

count the experimental Dennis Dominator built for South Yorkshire PTE in 1984.

After 1970 the decline of the trolleybus was rapid. Only Bradford, Cardiff, Teesside and Walsall survived into that decade – Cardiff and Walsall (actually West Midlands PTE by this time) only just as they had both closed down trolleybus operation by October. This left just Teesside, which finally abandoned trolleybuses in 1971, and Bradford,

notable as being one of the 1911 pioneers, which closed its system in March 1972.

There have been schemes to re-establish trolleybus operation in the UK, notably in Yorkshire, but no scheme appears to have got much further than the drawing-board. ♠

The last new batch of trolleybuses built for service in Britain were Sunbeam MF2B built between
1958 and 1962 with Weymann two-door bodies. A 1958 example is seen at the trolleybus turntable at
Christchurch. The newest buses were only seven years old when the system closed in 1969.
P Poulter

THE single-deck bus got a boost in the 1960s when the maximum dimensions were further relaxed in 1961. Now buses could be up to 36ft long and 8ft 2½in wide, and while this applied to all types of bus, the potential for 36ft single-deckers was quickly recognised. If the 44-seaters of 1950 brought operators closer to double-deck capacity, the 53-55 seats that could be fitted into a 36ft bus allowed older double-deckers of the same capacity to be replaced without any loss of seating capacity. In addition, one-man operation was only allowed on single-deckers so operators wishing to make economies with driver-only buses had to go for higher-capacity single-deckers. What they didn't know at the time was that the rules would change during the decade and the double-decker would come back into favour.

Suddenly everybody was buying longer buses, though not everybody went for the full legal length. An intermediate length of around 32ft virtually replaced the 30ft length for operators requiring shorter buses. Similarly double-deckers got longer, but generally to 31-32ft.

AEC and Leyland were first to introduce 36ft single-deck chassis. AEC stretched its Reliance and offered a new bigger engine, the 9.6-litre AH590, while Leyland stretched the Leopard. This had been introduced in 1959, essentially a Tiger Cub chassis with the bigger O.600 engine, and sales had hardly been earth-shattering. But with the boost of the extra length the Leopard came into its own and became one of the most familiar chassis around.

The long Reliance and Leopard gave the manufacturers breathing space to look at alternative chassis layouts to take full advantage of the new length. Bristol, still building only for state-owned fleets, beat its rivals with the RE, which featured a horizontal engine mounted at the rear. The Gardner 10.45-litre 6HLX and Leyland 11.1-litre 680 were the engine choices, and the RE, as a bus and as a coach, proved to be a very sound design.

The Leyland Panther was one of the rather unsuccessful breed of new rear-engined chassis introduced in the 1960s. Southport Corporation operated this 1968 example with Metro-Cammell 45-seat two-door body.

Iain MacGregor

Sunderland Corporation bought a range of the first-generation rear-engined types for its move to driver-only operation and its notorious flat fare token scheme. It bought Leyland Panthers, as seen here, as well as AEC Swifts, Bristol REs and Daimler Roadliners. Bodywork was to Sunderland's design, in this case by Strachans.
Arnold Richardson/ Photobus

One of the more unusual rear-engined designs was the Albion Viking VK43, a lighter-weight model designed primarily for the Scottish Bus Group companies, which were the main customers; they were useful for rural and other less-demanding duties. All SBG's Vikings carried Alexander Y-type bodywork similar to that on this 1969 Alexander (Northern) example.
Arnold Richardson/ Photobus

Bedford adopted a more unusual approach to the 36ft length. The VAL model, introduced in 1962, had small-diameter wheels and twin-steering front axles, and while it was most popular as a coach, several operators took VALs with bus bodies seating up to 55 passengers.

Ford, which had replaced Commer as Bedford's deadliest rival for the lightweight market, managed to design its 1963 Thames 36 model as a two-axle model. Like the VAL it had a front-mounted engine.

It was 1964 before more 36ft models appeared. AEC, Daimler and Leyland all chose the Commercial Motor Show that year to unveil new models, none of which were to prove as successful as the mid-underfloor engined chassis.

AEC's offering was the Swift with a horizontal AEC engine at the rear, either the 8.25-litre AH505 or the 11.3-litre AH691. The Swift sold well, particularly to London Transport (where the bigger-engined chassis was known as the Merlin), but dissatisfaction with reliability led to early withdrawals.

Leyland's rear-engined chassis, sharing the Swift's chassis frame following the merger of the two great rivals in 1962, was the Panther with Leyland's faithful O.600 engine, and there was a shorter (33ft) brother, the Panther Cub, with the 6.54-litre O.400.

Weak point

On its Roadliner Daimler opted for a compact engine that

was unfamiliar to British operators, the 9.6-litre Cummins V6-200, and this unit was to prove the weak point in what was otherwise a sound chassis. Resistance to the Roadliner prompted Daimler to introduce a single-deck version of its Fleetline in 1966 with transverse rear engine and this sold in respectable numbers over the next eight years, often to operators attracted by the prospect of a standard chassis for both single-deck and double-deck types.

Not all 1960s single-deckers were rear-engined. Bedford's VAM range, from 1965 was another front-engined model with a setback front axle, and was to 32-33ft length. Bedford chassis had always been used for bus, as distinct to coach, duties, but models like the VAM which allowed one-man operation attracted a number of larger operators to Bedfords. Ford's rival chassis was the R192 introduced in 1965.

Other builders had less success with lighter front-engined chassis. Albion introduced the Viking VK41L in 1963, and Dodge the S306/307 models in 1962, but neither model set the heather on fire.

BMMO meantime was continuing to do its own thing. A succession of underfloor-engined models during the 1950s

had seen the company moving to integral construction, disc brakes, independent front suspension, and to the longer 36ft models from 1962 with the S16. Later models had a bigger 10.5-litre BMMO engine mounted under the floor, for BMMO resisted the lure of the rear engine.

Double-deck development continued with new rear-engined models, but there were still new front-engined designs to appear. The first of these was the Albion Lowlander, Leyland's susprisingly late entry in the Lodekka-type stakes. A lowheight version of the Titan PD3 developed mainly for the Scottish Bus Group, the Lowlander (usually badged as a Leyland outside Scotland) was built for only five years.

The limited response to the integral Bridgemaster persuaded AEC to offer a lowheight chassis, the Renown, from 1962. Although it was a better-regarded bus, only 252 Renowns were built, no doubt reflecting its late entry to the market.

The Dennis Loline had reached its MkIII (and final) version by 1960; this was an improved version allowing a flatter floor.

Guy introduced its Arab V in 1962, a lower-height chassis

A very different type of rear-engined single-decker, based on the double-deck Leyland Atlantean chassis. Portsmouth Corporation was one of only three customers for single-deck Atlanteans, though Daimler enjoyed some success with a single-deck Fleetline, arguing the benefits of fleet standardisation. The bus shown, new in 1971, has bodywork by Seddon.
Arnold Richardson/Photobus

Top: **Bedfords and Fords were bought by several of the territorial companies looking for cheaper, lighter and more economical vehicles to run on less demanding services. Scottish Bus Group companies bought both types; this is a 1968 Eastern Scottish Bedford VAM70 with 41-seat Willowbrook body working on a local service into Edinburgh in 1975.**
Iain MacGregor

Above: **Unusually for a municipal fleet in a busy urban area, Wolverhampton Corporation bought this Ford R226 with Strachans 54-seat bodywork in 1966. It is seen in Wolverhampton in 1970 still in Corporation colours but with new West Midlands fleetnames reflecting the change of control in 1969.**
Iain MacGregor

which allowed for a more suitable forward entrance; it was one of the last conventional front-engined double-deck chassis to remain on the market, until 1968.

BMMO, ever adventurous, had different thoughts on double-deck design in the 1960s. Having put the first underfloor-engined single-deckers into production immediately after the war, it now turned to thoughts of an underfloor double-decker. AEC had briefly dabbled with this concept, but BMMO built two D10 prototypes in 1960/1, though no more followed.

The demise of long-running chassis like the AEC Regent, Daimler CV, Guy Arab and Leyland Titan – all of which disappeared from the model lists in 1968/9 – was a consequence of two things: the Bus Grants scheme and the rear-engined double-decker.

The Bus Grants scheme was conceived to encourage operators to buy new vehicles suitable for one-man operation by paying intially 25% and eventually 50% of the purchase price of approved types as a grant. The front-engined double-decker was not on the approved list, so the rear-engined chassis were king.

After the Atlantean, Daimler was hot on Leyland's heels with its Fleetline chassis, introduced in 1960. The Fleetline, with the Gardner 6LX engine mounted transversely at the rear, had a similar layout to the Atlantean but offered a true lowheight layout thanks to a dropped-centre rear axle. This proved attractive to company operators with low

bridge problems, and Daimlers, traditionally regarded as municipal buses, were soon figuring in a much wider range of fleets.

Bristol soldiered on with its Lodekka until 1968, when it was replaced by the new VRT. The VR type had first appeared in 1966 with an in-line engine mounted in the rear offside corner, the VRL, but operator resistance led Bristol to rework it as the VRT with a more conventional transverse engine. The VRT was altogether more successful than the VRL, and remained in production until 1981 selling to the Tilling and Scottish Groups, to the National Bus Company, and to a wide range of municipal, PTE and private companies.

Leyland's share deal with Bristol in 1965 brought Bristol chassis and ECW bodies back on to the open market; no longer were Bristol/ECW products restricted to state-owned companies and many fleets rushed to buy Bristols again. As the 1960s drew to a close the acquisition by the state Transport Holding Company (1963 successor to the British Transport Commission) of the BET group led to the creation of the giant National Bus Company which brought together the two big groups, BET and Tilling. This would have far-reaching consequences for the design of single-deck buses and the formation of the first Passenger Transport Executives (PTEs) would create a new breed of customer with immense buying power.

Further rationalisation

There was further rationalisation among the body-builders

Top: **Midland Red's last 30ft underfloor-engined single-deckers were the S15 class, built in 1962. These were integrally-built by BMMO as 40-seat dual-purpose vehicles, suitable for bus and express coach work, and featured disc brakes and rubber suspension.**
M Sutcliffe

Above: **Another Leyland group model developed for the Scottish Bus Group was the Albion Lowlander, essentially a lowheight Titan PD3. Many carried the very rounded style of Alexander forward-entrance bodywork seen on this 1963 Western SMT LR1 example.**
G Lumb

Top: **The BMMO D9 was the last double-deck model to go into production for Midland Red. Produced in quantity from 1960, the 30ft long D9 was integrally-built with rubber suspension and independent front suspension. This 1960 example has BMMO-built 72-seat bodywork. After the D9, and the two experimental D10 underfloor-engined double-deckers, Midland Red turned to Daimler's Fleetline for its double-deck needs.**
Arnold Richardson/Photobus

Above: **Many early 36ft buses carried fairly uninspired body designs like this 1962 Leyland Leopard with 53-seat Willowbrook body, one of three supplied to the famous Winchester independent, King Alfred and seen at the familiar Broadway departure point in its home town in 1963.**
P R Wallis

The Alexander Y-type body was one of the first to take advantage of new materials and regulations that allowed one-piece wrap-round windscreens. The Y-type was available in small-windowed bus form, or, as here, on a 1969 Western SMT Leyland Leopard at Tarbert in 1971, with panoramic side windows.
Iain MacGregor

in the 1960s. Massey sold out to Northern Counties, Harrington stopped building bodies, Weymann closed down at Addlestone; but there were new entrants too, notably Cambridge-based Marshall, which quickly established itself in the market.

Alexander, ECW, East Lancs, MCW, Marshall, Northern Counties, Park Royal-Roe and Willowbrook tended to compete for business, and while operators often had their favoured bodybuilders, keen price competition meant that valuable new customers could be won.

Alexander had expanded beyond its Scottish roots, particularly after it opened its new Falkirk factory in 1958. Now it was winning business from municipal and BET group companies as well. ECW was still only building for the state sector at the start of the 1960s but after the 1965 Leyland share exchange it could compete for any business and build on any chassis. East Lancs, Northern Counties and Willowbrook had limited bodybuilding capacity, but each had a group of faithful customers. MCW continued to look for big orders from home and export customers and was often involved in substantial contracts that tied up capacity for long periods. Park Royal-Roe passed into the Leyland Motor Corporation following the merger with ACV in 1962 and increasingly built on Leyland group chassis; Park Royal-Roe, and to a degree ECW, became Leyland's in-house bodybuilders and customers were encouraged to consider 'one-stop shopping' from Leyland.

Body design changed dramatically in the 1960s, a combination of operator pressure, changes in regulations,

and the availability of new materials. Operator resistance to the boxy and unattractive early rear-engined double-deckers led to exciting new designs. The longer buses legalised from 1961 gave designers greater scope and a change to a minor Construction & Use regulation – which meant that the driver's windscreen did not need to open – allowed new shaped windscreens; this coupled with a much wider use of newer materials like glassfibre meant that designers could achieve shapes that would have been expensive and difficult using metal.

The first of the new breed of double-deck bodies came from MCW on Atlantean for Liverpool Corporation, and municipal one-upmanship may have encouraged other undertakings to pressurise their coachbuilders into more exciting designs. For Glasgow Corporation, Alexander came up with a new design using curved-glass screens at the front, a style that would be copied by other bodybuilders. Park Royal added peaks for Sheffield Transport to disguise its normal body, and Roe used peaks on Fleetlines for Sunderland Corporation. Edinburgh Corporation pioneered the use of panoramic windows on Alexander-bodied

Bodybuilders started to pay greater attention to double-deck design in the 1960s, often encouraged by operators, and this 1969 Sheffield Corporation Leyland Atlantean PDR2/1 (33ft long) carries a stylish Park Royal 79-seat two-door body. This basic style was widely used during the 1970s. It is seen at Bradford's Chester Street bus station in 1970.

H J Black

Atlanteans, and Roe used big windows to good effect on bodies for Leeds.

ECW, on the other hand, introduced a predictably-styled but undoubtedly competent body on the Bristol VRT.

As the 1960s drew to a close designs were emerging that would be developed into 1970s classics. Park Royal-Roe introduced a design in 1968 that would soon become very familiar throughout Britain, and Northern Counties produced a fairly uninspired design that would soon develop into another classic. Bolton Corporation had in 1966 developed a deep-windowed design with East Lancs, enhanced by a lighter livery, and this was another pointer to 1970s trends.

Probably the most significant new body design of the late 1960s was the Mancunian design for Manchester Corporation. Introduced in 1968 it was the first double-decker designed for driver-only operation and its dramatic styling represented a bold step forward in bus design.

Single-deck body design was almost as exciting. The first 36ft single-deck buses were fairly uninspired, but the BET group developed a standard design that was built for its fleet by a number of builders and soon became a standard for much of the industry. ECW's bodywork for the Bristol RE bus was undeniably a Lowestoft product but definitely a classic design. And Alexander went its own way with the curved-front Y-type, available with big windows and sloping pillars or with conventional side windows.

Single-deck buses had enjoyed a successful decade and falling passenger numbers meant that some operators had a much reduced need for double-deckers, finding 53 seats plus around 25 standees was as much capacity as they needed. The single-decker would continue to sell well through the 1970s but Leyland had a nasty surprise in store for the firms that specialised in building single-deck bus bodies. ♠

BROOMHOUSE LN.

223

DAIMLER

DDT 223H

6 We can work it out
The situation in London

London Transport tested 50 Leyland Atlanteans and eight Daimler Fleetlines in the 1960s; the Atlanteans were unsuccessful in London traffic but the Fleetlines led to further orders. One of the Fleetlines, with uninspired Park Royal bodywork, is seen during its short LT career. *J T Inglis*

L ONDON, they always insisted, is different. The problems faced by London Transport are different from those experienced in other parts of Britain. They needed different solutions, different approaches, different vehicles.

Of course up to a point they were right. If Birmingham, Glasgow and Manchester had traffic problems, then Central London's were worse and because London's problems were on Parliament's doorstep they were highly visible and a matter of official concern.

London Transport (LT) had been set up in 1933, bringing together bus, tramway, trolleybus and underground railway operators to form the first conurbation transport authority. The sheer size of the London Transport area was awe-inspiring, reaching out far into neighbouring counties, and a vast fleet of vehicles was needed to serve the millions living in the area. Some idea of the sheer scale of LT is given by figures for 1934, 1950 and 1970. The fleet (including trams

and trolleybuses where appropriate) rose from 8,597 in 1934 to 10,257 in 1950, but had dropped to 6,153 in 1970 following the hiving-off of London Country to NBC. Passenger journeys by LT surface vehicles in 1934 were 2,980 million, rising to 3,841 million in 1950, but down to less than half of that, 1,502 million, by 1970.

London had suffered badly in World War 2 and the LT fleet was pretty exhausted, with many vehicles suffering

58

Above: **A typical London scene for many years, a member of the RT family at Marble Arch. This is an RTL-type Leyland PD2, carrying a roofbox body as a consequence of London Transport's body-swap programme.**
Geoff Rixon

Left: **Nearing the end of its London life, an RT in 1978, still looking good in the modern surroundings of Heathrow bus station, a tribute to a 40-year old design.**
Stewart J Brown

from damage, lack of maintenance, or just plain old age. LT would normally have bought several hundred new buses each year between 1939 and 1945, but in fact only received 150 RTs, a few unfrozen buses, and 735 non-standard utility types. So its 8,000-plus bus fleet was desperately in need of updating. And of course LT still had trams (until 1952) and trolleybuses.

But for the war LT would have had one of the most up-to-date motorbus fleets in the country. Its revolutionary AEC Regent RT type bus, first seen in 1939, was widely admired and provided pointers to the future of bus design, but only 150 could be placed in service before the pressures of war forced production to cease. After the war LT placed substantial orders for RTs, but these were slow to get going

at a time when manufacturers were working flat out to get buses built.

Stopgap

As a stopgap LT took some non-standard AEC and Leyland single-deckers and double-deckers, but RTs started flowing through in 1947 (in 1950 alone, LT took delivery of just under 2,000 new buses) and by the time the last of the RT family had been placed in service it had grown to 6,956 buses. There were 4,825 AEC Regents with bodies by a range of builders, mostly to a common design, and there were 1,631 Leyland PD2s (RTLs) adapted to take RT bodies, plus another 500 8ft wide PD2s (RTWs). The RT was designed to suit LT's impressive overhaul system where the interchangeable bodies were removed from chassis which eventually emerged with a different body.

The RT family served London well for many years – the last operated for LT in 1979 – and for the best part of the 1950s there seemed to be little else on the Capital's streets. The influx of RTs allowed older and non-standard buses to be sold. The wartime utilities, sold when some were barely ten years old, were a popular buy for operators throughout the UK, many of whom had the vehicles rebodied or rebuilt for many more years' service.

The single-deck equivalent of the RT was the RF, built on AEC Regal IV underfloor-engined chassis. The RFs had solidly-built bodies by MCCW and gave many years of good service to London. And for lightly-loaded country routes LT turned to Guy for a special normal-control chassis, on which ECW built 26-seat bodies, the 84-strong GS class.

With the withdrawal of the trams complete LT decided to withdraw its trolleybuses and replace them with motorbuses. Not just any motorbus, not even an RT, but an entirely new breed of bus that would take the RT concept forward and offer something close to the 70 seats of the trolleybuses. The last RTs had still to be placed in service when LT unveiled its 'bus of the future', the Routemaster. Here was a bus conceived within the legal dimensions of the time, but offering 64 seats and a revolutionary approach to double-deck design.

The Routemaster (RM) 'chassis' was really two subframes built into an integral body (production versions were all built by Park Royal), and among its advanced features were independent front suspension, coil springing, power steering, a fully-automatic gearbox, and hydraulic braking. The bodywork had traces of the RT design but was generally crisp and modern, with an attractive front-end

Top: **Two green RTs at Stevenage bus station in London Country days, still essentially in LT livery but with the London Country fleetname and 'wheelbarrow' logo.**
G Lumb

Above: **Although London tried a 30ft forward entrance Routemaster unsuccessfully, the fleet provided for British European Airways to link central London with Heathrow Airport comprised 65 RMAs, shorter-length forward entrance examples which towed a luggage trailer. This one is seen in Cromwell Road, near the air terminal, in 1972.**
Iain MacGregor

The single-deck equivalent of the RT was the RF, an AEC Regal IV with Metro-Cammell bodywork. The Green Line RFs were most effectively refurbished in the 1960s to give these solid buses a longer lifespan. Newly out from overhaul, this RF is seen passing Craven House at Hampton Court.
Geoff Rixon

treatment. The prototype, RM1, was first shown in 1954 and entered experimental service in 1956, but LT's typically thorough development programme meant that it was 1958/9 before production RMs were seen and placed in service. The class grew to 2,760, comprising 2,123 27ft 6in RMs, 524 30ft RMLs, 69 27ft 6in RMC coaches, and 43 RCL 30ft coaches. In addition there was one RMF, a forward-entrance 30ft bus, and FRM1, the experimental rear-engined Routemaster. The Routemaster was offered on the open market and others were built – 65 27ft 6in forward-entrance buses for BEA airport services, and 50 30ft forward-entrance buses for Northern General.

Some felt that the Routemaster's long gestation period – designed in an era of 27ft long front-engined buses but introduced into a world of 30ft long rear-engined buses – meant that it was obsolete almost before it entered service, but the RM is undoubtedly an all-time classic bus and the fact that many have completed more than 35 years' service in London traffic and enjoyed latter-day success competing on the streets of several major British towns and cities does suggest LT knew what it was doing.

The Routemaster allowed London to withdraw all of its

trolleybus services between 1959 and 1962, bringing the world's largest trolleybus system to an end after a lifespan of just 31 years.

To the dismay of many the RM was to be the last LT bus to be designed from the ground up, although there were design exercises in the 1980s that could have heralded a new breed of London bus. Instead LT found itself turning to proprietary off-the-shelf products, though admittedly heavily London-ised ones, and it seemed that this was when its troubles started.

While the Routemasters were still entering service – the last were delivered in 1968 – LT decided to buy batches of other types to test them in London service. Although the rear-engined Routemaster was under development, LT turned to Daimler and Leyland for batches of Fleetlines

Above: **Crowds gather outside Fulwell garage for the last day of London trolleybuses in 1962. A 1939 L3 class AEC/MCW integral trolleybus sets out on the 667 route.**
Geoff Rixon

Left: **London's newest trolleybuses were the Q1 class, BUT 9641Ts with Metro-Cammell bodies supplied between 1948 and 1952; all had been withdrawn by 1961, and most were sold for further service with Spanish operators**

(eight) and Atlanteans (50). These had fairly uninspired Park Royal bodies and were used in the Central and Country area fleets. The Atlanteans were not successful and were sold to Hong Kong in 1973, where they ran until 1979/80; the Fleetlines led to further orders.

The other experimental vehicles were 14 AEC Reliance coaches for Green Line service and, most controversially, six AEC Merlins for one-man urban services carrying a high proportion of standing passengers. The Merlins, a big-engined version of the rear-engined AEC Swift, entered service in 1966 with Strachans bodies. These were the first of the now-familiar Red Arrows, linking mainline railway stations with other parts of central London. They operated on a flat-fare basis, passengers placing the exact fare in a slot to release a turnstile. The front portion of the two-door bus had space for 48 standees, and there were seats for 25

at the rear. Although the Merlins turned out to be unsuccessful in London service, the Red Arrow concept survives to this day.

Reshaping

Looking to the future London Transport produced a report *Reshaping London's Bus Services* which addressed the many problems facing LT – continuing passenger decline, acute traffic congestion, the shortage of suitable staff – and decided that shorter routes, more driver-only operation, and standee buses could work. While most other British

The first of the experimental LT Red Arrow AEC Merlins with Strachans bodywork at Victoria bus station on the original 500 service that linked Victoria with Waterloo.
G Lumb

cities were looking to the future with a new breed of driver-only double-deckers, London plumped for single-deckers and from 1968 placed in service 659 more AEC Merlins and 700 of the smaller-engined AEC Swift.

This turned out to be one of LT's poorer decisions and the Merlins and Swifts had very short lives in London service. For its next generation of bus London turned back to double-deckers and chose Daimler's Fleetline.

But before the Fleetlines started to arrive, London's Transport had gone through a major reorganisation. On 1 January 1970 the vast LT area was split in two: the Central area passed into the control of the London Transport Board, responsible to the Greater London Council, and the Country area and Green Line services were grouped together under a new company, London Country Bus Services, a subsidiary of the newly-formed National Bus Company.

LT had lost the problems of the country area but still had to face up to London's chronic traffic problems and a fleet of buses that was proving troublesome to run. The well-proved RTs and RMs continued to give reliable service – and many of the RTs were well over 20 years' old by this time – but the newer rear-engined AEC single-deckers were a different matter.

London Country did not have its troubles to seek. It served an awkward area ringing Greater London, and had inherited a fleet of newer buses designed primarily for Central London work though it lacked LT's sophisticated maintenance and overhaul facilities. Although London Country's ancestry would be obvious for many years to come, after a brief period in a green/yellow livery its buses would start to appear in standard National Bus corporate style and its vehicle orders would be for NBC standard types. ♠

The Metropolitan was one of the first overseas threats to Leyland's dominance in the double-deck market. Built by MCW around a Scania BR111DH underframe, it sold in respectable numbers, with Tyne & Wear PTE and London Transport as its biggest customers. A 1977 Tyne & Wear Metropolitan is seen outside Newcastle Central station. *Gavin Booth*

IT HAD all seemed very healthy in the 1950s with a suitably wide range of bus chassis and body manufacturers competing for the business. There already were some links, of course: AEC had taken over Crossley and Maudslay, neither still producing chassis by the end of the 1950s, and coachbuilders Park Royal and Roe. Leyland had started its expansion in a very modest way with the acquisition of Albion in 1951. But there were changes ahead.

AEC and Leyland, the two firms that had dominated the British bus industry for so many years, merged in 1962 and soon the Leyland Motor Corporation was born. Leyland had already started on its 1960s takeover trail with Standard-Triumph in 1961 and followed this with Rover in 1967.

In parallel with this Jaguar Cars had acquired Daimler in 1960, then Guy the following year. The enlarged Jaguar merged with British Motor Corporation in 1966 to form British Motor Holdings (BMH).

Pressure from government brought Leyland and BMH together in 1968 as British Leyland Motor Corporation (BLMC), a vast organisation controlling a substantial part of the British car and commercial vehicle industry. The bus, truck and van companies were generally in a healthier

condition than the car businesses and over the next decade the commercial vehicle builders were starved of investment while BLMC attempted to restore the fortunes of the ailing British car industry. The subsequent stream of sub-standard cars and the music-hall jokes about BLMC's poor productivity and union problems did nothing for the once-trusted Leyland name.

Not that everything was perfect in BLMC's Truck & Bus Division. Finding itself with a model list containing previously competing chassis the company set about eliminating duplication. The remaining front-engined double-deckers (AEC Regent V, Bristol Lodekka, Daimler CV, Guy Arab V and Leyland Titan PD2/PD3) went in 1968, hastened no doubt by their ineligibility for Bus Grants; the AEC Swift, Daimler Roadliner, and Leyland Tiger Cub and Panther all went soon – again there was an

Top: **Seventeen years separate these two Ipswich Corporation buses, demonstrating the advances in double-deck design. On the right is a 1956 AEC Regent III with 61-seat Park Royal body, and passing it is a 1973 Leyland Atlantean with 71-seat Roe body. Although Ipswich had been a staunch AEC fan from its first motorbus purchases in 1950, the lack of an AEC double-decker meant that it had to turn elsewhere.**
Gavin Booth

Above: **The Leyland-Bristol share exchange in 1965 brought Bristol chassis and ECW bodies back on to the open market, and many operators became keen customers. Great Yarmouth Corporation opted for what were essentially standard NBC ECW-bodied 77-seat VRTs in 1977/8.**
Gavin Booth

ulterior motive (this time the Leyland National) for the withdrawal of the rear-engined chassis.

Models that continued were the single-deck AEC Reliance, Bristol LH and RE, and Leyland Leopard, and the three rear-engined double-deckers, the Bristol VRT, Daimler Fleetline and Leyland Atlantean. The Bristol RE outlived its former stablemates partly because of orders from Ulsterbus/Citybus, but the Leyland National was waiting in the wings to be BLMC's single-deck citybus. The underfloor-engined AEC Reliance and Leyland Leopard continued to satisfy coach and bus orders, particularly from operators like Scottish Bus and Ulsterbus who tended to be anti-National. The Bristol LH, introduced in 1967 as a lightweight underfloor chassis, would remain in the lists for some time, selling in bus and coach forms.

Next generation

The three double-deckers figured in Leyland's short-term plans, particularly as demand built up in the 1970s, but already thought was being given to the next generation. The Atlantean, on the market since 1958, was beginning to seem long in the tooth; the Fleetline had established itself as a

formidable rival during the 1960s; and the VRT, still very new, had been rushed into production and would need attention to improve the breed.

The Atlantean was first to receive the treatment, and the improved AN68 model with Leyland's 680 engine tackled the problems that had beset some of the earlier PDR-series chassis. An improved VRT appeared in 1974 and Leyland announced that the Fleetline would be phased out – though in practice it remained available until 1980. This was a signal to other builders who set about designing Fleetline replacements.

But Leyland was facing other problems. It had a virtual monopoly of the full-size bus market and many operators

Above: **Seddon made one of its periodic returns to the bus-building market with the rear-engined RU model, with Gardner engine. This RU with Seddon's own Pennine Coachcraft 47-seat body, was bought in 1972 by Lytham St Annes Corporation and is seen working for its successor, Fylde Borough.** *Gavin Booth*

Left: **The Seddon Pennine 4.236 was better known as the Midi, an early attempt to provide a small bus with big bus characteristics. Selnec PTE was a good customer, and this 1974 Midi has a 19-seat body, with space for a further 19 standees, and is being used on the frequent Centreline services linking Victoria and Piccadilly railway stations in Manchester.** *Gavin Booth*

were very uneasy about this, fearing that the situation could be abused in terms of prices or restricted choice.

The first challenge had come in 1969 when MCW had teamed up with the Swedish builder Scania to produce the Metro-Scania, a single-deck citybus based on the Scania BR111. MCW did this partly to protect its single-deck business which was under threat from Leyland's decision to standardise on the integral National. The Metro-Scania introduced a new sophistication to British buses, but sold only 133 between 1969 and 1973.

The MCW/Scania relationship also produced the Metropolitan double-decker in 1973, and around the same time Volvo dealer Ailsa Trucks developed the front-engined Ailsa double-decker. These were the first threats to Leyland's double-deck monopoly, and both models sold respectably, the Ailsa being particularly popular in its native Scotland.

Another significant Swedish model to appear in Britain was the Volvo B58, representing Volvo's first attempt at the British bus and coach market. After a slow start the B58 established itself with operators throughout the country, and paved the way for the infinitely more successful B10M.

Of the smaller British builders Seddon had its rear-engined RU, the little Midi, and the mid-engined Pennine VII; Dennis was still showing little interest in the bus market but in 1977 introduced its new Dominator double-decker.

Bedford and Ford, built in Britain by American-owned firms, were finding a broader range of customers for their lighter-weight chassis.

Leyland's answer to the Metropolitan and Ailsa, and its planned replacement for the Atlantean/Fleetline/VRT, was the B15, later named the Titan, an advanced integral double-decker featuring independent front suspension and hydraulic brakes. London was a target customer for the Titan and LT bought 1,164 examples. Other customers were less enthusiastic about the advanced specification and only 34 others were built. The Titan had an unhappy production history, starting at Park Royal in London, then moving to Workington, but not before ECW had rejected the chance to build it.

With most operators cool towards the Titan, Leyland had to keep its older double-deckers going for a few more years while it designed a new chassis that would eventually emerge as the Olympian, happily a much more succesful model.

Leyland's rationalisation continued and in the 1970s saw the final closure of the historic AEC factory at Southall and the end of of the road for the popular and long-running AEC Reliance. ♠

Opposite left: **The Dennis Dominator was designed as a Fleetline replacement, and enjoyed reasonable success in its 18-year production life. Many carried East Lancs bodies, and this 1981 example was built for Accrington-based Hyndburn Transport and carries that undertaking's distinctive blue/red livery.**
H J Black

Above: **The front-engined Ailsa represented a different approach to double-deck design, with its compact front-mounted Volvo engine. This is the prototype working in Glasgow in 1974 as a demonstrator for Alexander (Midland) and carrying that company's livery. Like many Ailsas it carries Alexander bodywork.**
Iain MacGregor

Right: **One of the prototype Leyland Titans, a 1977 demonstrator in London Transport red but working for Fishwick of Leyland. After being on extended loan this and another Titan prototype joined the Fishwick fleet.**
Stewart J Brown

Created in the second wave of PTEs, West Yorkshire PTE ran for a number of years under the MetroBus name, also worn by company buses in the area. Note the combined Metro and NBC logos on the front panel of this PTE Roe-bodied Fleetline, one of a large fleet of similar Atlanteans and Fleetlines bought between 1974 and 1980. This bus is strictly a Leyland Fleetline, model FE30AGR, built after production switched from Coventry to Leyland.

Stewart J Brown

A T VARIOUS TIMES there had been proposals for a network of regional transport boards covering. Britain, co-ordinating all operators in designated areas. This came nearest to fruition with the creation of the first Passenger Transport Authorities (PTAs) in 1969/70. The 1968 Transport Act which did so much to shape buses and bus companies in the 1970s and early 1980s, set up the first PTAs in the West Midlands, in the Manchester area, on Merseyside and on Tyneside. The PTAs had powers to plan, co-ordinate and organise public transport in their designated areas. This meant that local bus services, out-of-town bus services, and rail services were all affected by the new organisation.

At a stroke 20 municipal bus fleets found themselves absorbed into the new Passenger Transport Executives (PTEs) which ran the day-to-day operations. Three of the largest municipal undertakings found themselves at the heart of the new PTEs.

The first to be set up was West Midlands PTE, on 1 October 1969; this combined the Birmingham, Walsall, West Bromwich and Wolverhampton fleets (nearly 2,000 buses) and opted for a fleet livery largely based on Birmingham's blue/cream.

Selnec (South-east Lancashire, north-east Cheshire) PTE was set up on 1 November 1969 and had the biggest fleet, over 2,500 buses from 11 municipalities – Ashton, Bolton, Bury, Leigh, Manchester, Oldham, Ramsbottom, Rochdale, SHMD Board, Salford and Stockport. Selnec chose a distinctive orange/white livery.

A month later Merseyside PTE combined the Birkenhead, Liverpool and Wallasey fleets, some 1,300 buses, and painted them green/cream in Liverpool and blue/cream in Wirral.

The last of the first PTEs was the smallest, Tyneside, with just over 400 buses from the Newcastle and South Shields fleets. Tyneside opted for a yellow/cream livery based on the Newcastle colours.

Although the PTEs had no powers of compulsory puchase of other operators, the new regime had a significant impact on the company and private operators in the designated areas. Some of these, operating longer-distance services beyond the PTE boundaries, were not greatly affected, but others earned significant and often highly profitable revenue from services wholly

Tyneside, and later Tyne & Wear, PTE adopted a livery based on the Newcastle Corporation scheme. This 1979 Leyland Atlantean AN68A/2R seen in Newcastle has Metro-Cammell 86-seat bodywork and after only three years was sold to Northern General with a number of similar vehicles when the PTE found itself with a surplus of buses following the opening of the Metro system. At the time Tyne & Wear was one of the small number of fleets still favouring 33ft long double-deckers.
Gavin Booth

or mainly in the PTE areas and were anxious to protect their revenue.

The first move came at Selnec when it acquired the services of the North Western company in the PTE area in 1972; other parts of North Western went to the Crosville and Trent companies.

Heartland

In West Midlands, Midland Red was the operator most affected and many were surprised when in 1973 it sold its services in the area to the PTE, along with over 400 buses. The loss of its heartland seemed to destabilise the rest of the Midland Red company, which faced a number of difficult years until it was split four ways in 1981.

The situation on Tyneside was rather different, where the principal NBC companies, United and particularly the Northern group, had something like half of the

market. Take-overs were not the answer and agency agreements were entered into with a vast range of joint ticketing arrangements and eventually a proprtion of the United and Northern fleets in PTE yellow/white.

One situation facing all of the new PTEs was fleet replacement. With an inheritance of buses representing the individuality, even quirkiness, of municipal operators, and a situation where fleet replacement had slowed

West Midlands PTE took over a large fleet of Daimler Fleetlines with the Coventry undertaking in 1974. This 1971 model has East Lancs 72-seat two-door body.
Gavin Booth

down as Corporations prepared to lose their bus services, new standardised buses were needed quickly. Often the preferences of the dominant municipality carried the day, so West Midlands continued to buy Daimler Fleetlines and Merseyside and Tyneside Leyland Atlanteans. But there were concessions like Fleetlines for Merseyside's Wirral operations.

Selnec had the most mixed fleet with buses from eight different chassis manufacturers, and set about buying batches of experimental vehicles to find its ideal standards. Fleets like Bolton and Manchester had led the way in the design of attractive modern double-deckers,

and when the new-style Selnec double-decker appeared in 1972 it was no surprise that it was a good-looking, well-considered design. Selnec's vehicle requirements were so great that over 1,800 standards entered service between 1972 and 1984 on Atlantean and Fleetline chassis.

But at the same time Selnec (and from 1974 its successor, Greater Manchester) was trying other double-

deck types, like the Ailsa, Dennis Dominator, Foden-NC, Scania-MCW Metropolitan, and single-deckers like the Leyland National, Metro-Scania and Seddon Midi. In 1973 it even turned to Mercedes-Benz for two 0305 underframes on which were mounted Northern Counties bodies; they were to remain unique in Britain.

Scotland's only PTE was Greater Glasgow, formed in June 1973 around the 1,281-bus Glasgow Corporation fleet.

More PTEs were set up in 1974 at the time of local government reorganisation in England and Wales. South Yorkshire PTE, with nearly 1,000 buses, took over from the municipal fleets at Doncaster, Rotherham and Sheffield; West Yorkshire PTE, with almost 1,500 buses, took over at Bradford, Halifax/Calderdale, Huddersfield and Leeds.

At the same time the creation of new metropolitan counties brought changes at the existing PTEs. Merseyside was extended to take in the St Helens and Southport undertakings. Selnec became Greater Manchester and gained Wigan; Tyneside became Tyne & Wear with Sunderland added. And West Midlands gained Coventry. The new and enlarged PTEs now had around 11,200 buses between them, and the number of municipal operators had dropped drastically, from 91 in

Top: **Greater Glasgow PTE** kept its vehicle-buying options open and chose Volvo Ailsas as well as **MCW** Metrobuses and Leyland Olympians in the early 1980s. The first of its 1981 batch of Ailsas, with Alexander R-type bodywork, is pursued by one of its first batch of Metrobuses. They wear the post-1980 **GGPTE** livery with Trans-Clyde fleetnames, which was replaced by Strathclyde Buses' orange.
Gavin Booth

Above: **South Yorkshire PTE** was an early advocate of articulated buses, and its first generation artics consisted of **MANs**, like this bus, and **Leyland-DABs**. Licensing problems meant that they had to provide a free service on the City Clipper route – the first use of artics on public service in Britain. They were short-lived with **SYPTE**, though a second generation of Leyland-DAB artics has since been bought.
Gavin Booth

1969 to just 51 in 1974, with a total fleet of some 6,200 buses. The local government changes in England and Wales brought a range of new names (and sometimes liveries) for many of the former Corporation and UDC undertakings, now owned by Borough councils.

In Scotland local government reorganisation took place a year later, and the three remaining Corporation bus fleets passed into the control of their local Regional Councils.

New breed

In the PTE and municipal fleets the once all-powerful double-decker was being challenged by the new breed of single-decker. Between 1966 and 1980 the double-deck:single-deck ratio had changed from 93:7 to 79:21 as operators changed their buying policies. Some fleets stuck resolutely to double-deckers and some went wholeheartedly for single-deckers, but an increasing number recognised that large-capacity single-deckers had a part to play and bought both types.

Availability was one factor. The industrial relations problems of the early 1970s meant that chassis and body manufacturing capacity had got well out of step – at one time there were thousands of buses stuck in the system, chassis waiting for bodies, body capacity but no chassis. Operators desperate for new buses took what they could get and this helped models like the integral

mass-produced Leyland National. It also boosted new single-deck models like the Metro-Scania and Seddon RU.

The PTE fleets tended to be innovative when it came to vehicle design. In addition to developing their own standard models they were prepared to experiment with new concepts like the battery buses used by Greater Manchester and the articulated buses used by South Yorkshire. The battery buses were hampered by the weight of the batteries and the limited mileage range and never progessed past the experimental stage. The artics were bought for service in Sheffield, five MAN and five Leyland-DAB, but while artics are very popular elsewhere in the world they have never taken off in Britain. ♠

Buying secondhand buses was something that was once unheard of among the major municipal fleets, but with bargains like ex-London DMS-type Fleetlines on the market, even West Midlands PTE found it difficult to resist. A 10-year old DMS, converted to single-door layout, is seen in 1982.
Gavin Booth

The Leyland National is probably the greatest legacy of the influence of the National Bus Company, a bold venture with British Leyland to mass-produce a standardised rear-engined single-decker. The B-series National was an attempt to provide a simpler, cheaper National for less demanding duties. A Crosville example is seen in 1981 at Tanygrisiau, in full NBC corporate green livery.

A Moyes

Very much the standard **NBC** double-decker of the 1970s, a 1974 ex-City of Oxford Bristol **VRT** with ECW body, seen in Perranporth in 1983 in the fleet of Western National and carrying Cornwall Busways local identity.
John Robinson

1 JANUARY 1969 was a significant day for the British bus industry. The state-owned company fleets that covered virtually all of mainland Britain were put under new control. The Tilling and BET groups, together in public ownership for the first time, were reorganised to form the National Bus Company (NBC), a giant organisation providing bus and coach services in most parts of England and Wales, with a staff of over 80,000 and a fleet of over 20,000 buses and coaches. These two very different organisations found themselves having to work together and onetime rivals were now forced to speak.

With 44 subsidiary companies in 1969, NBC quickly embarked on rationalisation which meant that some once-significant company names disappeared and others found that they were mere subsidiaries of a former rival.

NBC's initial fleet was fairly mixed. While the Tilling companies had been fed a diet of Bristol/ECW products, BET had given its companies greater autonomy and consequently there was much less standardisation. NBC had vested interests in vehicle manufacture – its shares in Leyland National and Bristol/ECW doubtless helped its buying decisions – and so the Leyland National quickly

National Bus turned to Willowbrook for bodywork on some Bristol VRTs in 1977, and Northern General received a batch with a lower front-end treatment that was based on the ECW design, but the rest of the body was rather more square.
Gavin Booth

became the group's single-deck standard and the Bristol VRT became the double-deck standard. But when supply and demand got out of step in the mid-1970s NBC turned to Leyland and Park Royal-Roe for Atlanteans. Less predictable were orders for 100 Seddon RU for Crosville in 1969 and 100 Ford R192 for Midland Red. The use of lightweight Bedfords and Fords was catching on among the larger fleets at this time, but the Midland Red order was by far the most significant.

NBC's vehicle standardisation was further emphasised by the adoption of a standard corporate livery style in 1972. This was essentially a development of the Tilling red and green liveries familiar in many parts of the country, but used new colours so that now most NBC buses were painted either poppy red or leaf green, sometimes with white relief, and fleetnames appeared in a standard white typeface supported by the NBC double-N logo. The imposition of standard liveries caused much wailing and gnashing of teeth among the subsidiary companies, and among the former BET fleets the livery diktat signalled the end of well-loved liveries like Ribble's crimson and Southdown's green.

It also meant that 'red' companies sometimes became 'green' companies and vice-versa and doubtless caused public confusion when two or more companies that had previously worn different shades and applications of, say, red, found themselves painted in identical liveries and using identical buses.

Around the same time NBC had painted all its express and touring coaches in white NATIONAL livery.

Rationalisation

The sheer size of NBC meant that some form of rationalisation was necessary. Fleets were grouped together into regions; some disappeared; others were merged. Like the PTEs, the size of NBC meant that it had the facilities to experiment and innovate. On the vehicle side, NBC

Northern General buses working within the Tyne & Wear PTE area were painted in a yellow/white livery, and this 1978 example with normal-height ECW bodywork, seen in South Shields, is fitted with the Leyland 501 engine.
Gavin Booth

The NBC inheritance from BET group fleets was rather more mixed than the standardised Tilling buses. This 1964 Leyland-Albion Lowlander LR7 with Weymann 72-seat body wears full NBC poppy red livery. Note the painted-over side advert panel; illuminated adverts were a brief fashion in the 1960s. It is seen at Dewsbury in 1977.
H J Black

Even before it became part of **NBC**, Ribble had started buying Bristol REs and ECW bodywork shortly after these products came back on to the open market. This is the shorter-length **RESL6L** model, with Leyland engine, one of a 1972 batch of 40. It is seen at Preston's impressively-styled bus station, with Preston Borough Atlanteans in the background.
Gavin Booth

mounted trials of four current double-deck models: five each of Ailsa/Alexander and Scania-MCW Metropolitan, and four Bristol VRT/ECW (two with Gardner 6LXB and two with Leyland 510 engines) were tested by Maidstone & District from 1976.

NBC was also involved in testing a Foden-NC double-decker at Potteries, and a liquid petroleum gas Atlantean at Ribble. At Runcorn Crosville was running on a 12-mile Busway. At various fleets minibuses were being tested for specialised services, including the innovative village bus linking Norfolk villages and manned by volunteer drivers.

But all NBC's efforts could not stem the drop in passenger numbers – 46% between 1969 and 1984 – and so more drastic measures were required. Bus companies traditionally had a good 'feel' for the market but there was often a lack of good market research data. The Market Analysis Project (MAP) involved surveys of passenger movements to help planners identify travel patterns and design services appropriate to the time. Vehicle workings were tightened up to allow more economical use of expensive resources and a new style of promotional marketing was introduced to the bus industry with such innovations as local identities to encourage passenger loyalty and a much greater emphasis on publicity and information.

Scotland's buses changed on 1 January 1969, but to the outsider the change was less dramatic. Scottish Bus Group (SBG) moved from Transport Holding Company control in London to a new Scottish-based body, the Scottish Transport Group (STG). STG was more than just buses; it included the ferries of Caledonian Steam Packet and eventually David MacBrayne, and with the MacBrayne business came that company's bus services which were split between existing SBG companies.

SBG started with over 18,000 staff and nearly 4,900 buses and was a more traditional organisation than NBC. Its seven operating companies chose to buy fairly conservative buses which were sturdy and reliable, and economical to

Scottish Bus Group's dissatisfaction with early Bristol VRTs led to an exhange with NBC for FLF Lodekkas. An ex-Southern Vectis 1967 FLF with standard ECW 70-seat forward entrance bodywork, is seen in Edinburgh in 1973 working for Eastern Scottish, still with Tilling-style destination layout.
Iain MacGregor

run. So the Leyland Leopard was still the standard single-decker and in the absence of the Bristol FLF Lodekka, the Bristol VRT and Daimler Fleetline were the standard double-deckers – though the VRTs didn't last long after SBG and NBC agreed a swap with Lodekkas.

Like other operators at the time SBG was unhappy with Leyland's stranglehold on the new bus market and sought to find alternative suppliers. Leyland's inability to fit the Gardner engine to the Leopard led to the creation of the Seddon Pennine VII, essentially a Gardner-engined Leopard that allowed SBG to dual-source on single-deckers. And the search for a Lodekka successor produced the Ailsa, not quite what SBG had in mind, but a successful

model for which SBG was the principal customer.

For rural and other lighter duties SBG turned to Bedford and Ford, though apparently indiscriminate allocation to urban and express duties led to some problems.

SBG resisted the temptation to follow NBC along the

The Dennis Dorchester, essentially a Gardner-engined equivalent to the Leyland Tiger, was built largely for SBG, and a 1983 Central Scottish Dorchester with Alexander TE-style 49-seat dual purpose body is seen in East Kilbride.
Gavin Booth

corporate livery route, though a corporate fleetname style was adopted in 1978 and coaches on the prestige Scotland-London express services had appeared in a standard blue/white SCOTTISH livery in 1976.

SBG did follow NBC's lead when it chose to carry out its SCOTMAP market research exercises, based on NBC's earlier experience.

But both groups found themselves in many ways with rather less freedom than they had enjoyed in the 1950s and 1960s. Tilling and SBG had both been successful parts of the British Transport Commission and the Transport Holding Company, regularly returning healthy profits and running well-managed businesses. This meant that managers were allowed to run their companies without much interference and so it wasn't easy to adapt to the new regime following the local government reorganisations of 1974/5. Now Counties and Regions had a statutory voice in the provision of public transport services – some bus companies saw this as interference – but in return local authorities were able to subsidise loss-making services. There had been subsidy for bus operators in the past, for rural bus services for example, but this was the first time that widespread subsidies were available.

And bus operators needed them. The unstoppable growth of private motoring took its toll in bus ridership figures and the inflation and industrial relations problems of the 1970s added to the bus industry's problems.

Many argue that market research exercises like MAP should have been happening much sooner. While the state-owned bus companies were making money there never seemed to be much need to cut costs; now that the tide was turning many companies discovered that they had little idea what their real costs were. MAP helped them to do that and placed the state-owned companies in a stronger position to face the upheaval that the 1980s would bring. ♠

Above: **Local authority revenue support arrangements meant that fleets that had previously relied on secondhand and lightweight buses found themselves with good-quality new stock. Highland Scottish received this Leyland Olympian with Alexander RL-type lowheight bodywork in 1984, one of a batch of six. It is seen in Inverness.**
Gavin Booth

Below: **Symbolic of the changes that would soon change the face of the National Bus Company — a Devon General Bristol VRT/ECW in Exeter in 1981. Within a few years minibuses dominated the Exeter scene, and Devon General would be the first NBC bus company to pass into private ownership.**
Gavin Booth

The Dennis Dominator introduced new competition on to the double-deck market in the 1970s. This long Dominator with Northern Counties 85-seat body is seen at Gateshead in the fleet of the noted independent, OK Motor Services.
Gavin Booth

L EYLAND'S near-monopoly of full-size bus and coach models, following the mergers of the 1960s, was causing unease among some of its customers. There was no doubt that Leyland was in a strong position, particularly with the government's Bus Grants scheme encouraging an upsurge in orders for new buses. With AEC, Bristol, Daimler and Guy under its control, as well as bodybuilders ECW and Park Royal-Roe, Leyland's capacity for building new buses was unequalled.

Operators worried that Leyland would abuse its dominant position by restricting customer choice or by increasing prices – a temptation when, between 1971 and 1980, the government was picking up 50% of the cost of new buses.

Leyland had certainly cut its model lists, though the front-engined double-deckers were arguably on their last legs when the Bus Grants scheme finally killed them off. There were possibly fewer tears shed for the first-generation rear-engined single-deckers, but Leyland's replacement model would cause its fair share of controversy.

Top: **This was how many Leyland Nationals came off the production line at Workington – in NBC red, ready for fleetnames and numbers. This was the longer 11.3 metre version, in rarer two-door form.**
Gavin Booth

Above: **A typical NBC Leyland National one-door 49-seater, though wearing a commemorative livery, a welcome recognition of their heritage, by many companies. This bus carries the livery (though surely not the lettering) of the Mid-Cheshire Motor Bus Co, a fleet taken over by the North Western company in 1924.**
Policy Transport Photos

The **Daimler Fleetline continued to sell well through the 1970s. This 1972 Chester City Transport example, with Northern Counties 72-seat body, is seen outside Chester General station in 1973.**
Ron Robinson

The Leyland National, a joint venture between Leyland and the National Bus Company, was unlike anything that had been offered in Britain before. A special factory had been built near Workington in Cumbria to produce a highly-standardised rear-engined single-deck citybus on car-type production lines.

The British bus industry had always been fairly low-tech, with chassis and bodies built by hand by well-paid skilled craftsmen in what was a fairly labour-intensive exercise. The Workington plant was designed around the principle of assembling parts in a highly-mechanised factory using readily-available semi-skilled and unskilled labour.

After extensive testing the Leyland National was first shown to the world at the 1970 Commercial Motor Show. Here was a bus that looked very different to anything previously seen, available in just two lengths, 10.3m and 11.3m, and, it was suggested, in any colour as long as it was red or green. Operators who had been used to specifying their new buses right down to the type of ventilator or the colour of the seat moquette suddenly found that their choices were severely restricted. No longer could they pop along to their favoured coachbuilder to discuss the finer points of the body specification; Leyland was in effect saying 'take it or leave it'.

The bodybuilders who relied on single-deck business suddenly recognised the threat that the National and the lack of alternative chassis posed to their futures. MCW, Marshall and Willowbrook were three firms that had done well out of the single-deck bus market, and while Marshall turned to other markets including double-deckers, and Willowbrook to coaches and dual-purpose vehicles as well as double-deckers, MCW adopted a different strategy.

Liaison

MCW's liaison with Scania had produced the Metro-Scania single-decker in 1969 and the Metropolitan double-decker in 1973, and these together with double-deck orders kept the company busy during much of the 1970s. But it had got a taste for building complete buses and in 1978, in answer to Leyland's Titan, it introduced the successful Metrobus. This incorporated the Gardner 6LXB engine and Voith

The MCW-Scania Metropolitan enjoyed brief success on the UK market until MCW went it alone with its Metrobus model. This Metropolitan was one of 68 bought by Leicester City Transport between 1974 and 1977. Leicester also bought the single-deck Metro-Scania.
Stewart J Brown

automatic transmission, though later models used Rolls-Royce Eagle and Cummins L10 engines. The majority of Metrobuses were sold as complete MCW buses, but Alexander and Northern Counties also bodied the chassis. Some of the Alexander and MCW Metrobuses were semi-lowheight buses. London was an enthusiastic Metrobus customer, dual-sourcing with the Leyland Titan, and over 1,400 were placed in service. The other major customer was West Midlands PTE, with over 1,100.

In retrospect the introduction of the Leyland National in the early 1970s seems to have been a misjudgement. The mid-1960s interest in high-capacity single-deckers for driver-only operation had faded away in many fleets as driver-only double-deckers spread throughout Britain. Leyland said that its target was to produce 2,000 Nationals a year, though in practice it barely achieved half of that, and a major customer was inevitably the National Bus Company.

Nonetheless more that 7,000 Nationals were built in its 14-year production life and it won over some reluctant

customers, no doubt partly on account of its ready availability. There was concern at the choice of the unfamiliar fixed-head Leyland 8.2-litre 510 engine, and engine problems did earn earlier Nationals a poor reputation. But many of these buses, rebuilt or re-engined, are still giving useful service over 20 years' later. The slightly longer (10.6m/11.6m) National 2 appeared in 1979 with the bigger Leyland 680 engine, soon replaced by the 11.1-litre TL11H, and later Leyland bowed to pressure to offer Gardner engines.

Leyland's alternatives to the National were the mid-engined Reliance and Leopard, and the lighter Bristol LH, but operators were turning to other manufacturers to persuade them to build the chassis they wanted. The trouble was, there were very few of them. Outside Bedford and Ford, both small parts of multi-nationals who were heavily committed to making the best use of truck components, there was really only Seddon.

Seddon had never been a major force in the bus world. It had been building workmanlike bus chassis at Oldham alongside its mainstream trucks since 1946 but had not seemed to be interested in bulk orders. The RU chassis, introduced in 1969, was a first attempt to break into the big bus world. This was a rear-engined bus chassis with Gardner 6HLX engine, and some 250 were sold, the most notable deliveries being 100 for Crosville and 50 for Lancashire United Transport.

In 1972 Seddon developed a short-length version of its Pennine IV front-engined chassis, with Perkins 236 engine, fitted a bus body built by its coachbuilding arm, Pennine Coachcraft, and dubbed it the Midi.

For the Scottish Bus Group, frustrated that Leyland wouldn't offer a Gardner-engined Leopard, Seddon

Top: **London Transport was an enthusiastic customer for MCW's Metrobus model, and it dual-sourced Metrobuses and Leyland Titans for a number of years. This is a 1979 example.**
Stewart J Brown

Above: **The Foden-NC was another attempt to offer a double-deck chassis to pick up sales from former Fleetline customers. Only seven were bodied; four went to PTE fleets including this 1978 lowheight version for West Yorkshire PTE. Like all but one of the Fodens, it carries Northern Counties bodywork. It is seen at Huddersfield in 1977.**
H J Black

Some fleets continued to buy Bristol's **RE** chassis as long as they could, and it was popular with smaller municipal fleets. **Rossendale Borough bought four of these RESL6L with East Lancs bodies in 1975.**
Gavin Booth

developed the Pennine VII with mid-mounted Gardner 6HLXB engine and ZF gearbox. Some 500 were built between 1973 and 1982, the great majority for SBG fleets.

Dennis, a major force in today's bus market, was not really involved much in bus building after the Loline was discontinued in 1967. But with Leyland's decision to drop the Fleetline double-deck chassis , some operators were looking for a non-Leyland replacement. The Dennis answer in 1977 was the Dominator, with rear-mounted Gardner 6LXB engine – though subsequently a range of other engines has been fitted. Available in lowheight and normal height versions, the Dominator sold to a wide selection of customers in the municipal, PTE, state-owned and private sectors.

Leyland's monopoly was also threatened by Volvo's decision to sell its B58 mid-engined chassis in Britain. The AEC Reliance and Leyland Leopard had the mid-engined bus and coach market pretty well sewn up, and previously no real interest had been shown by European manufacturers. Volvo's B58 paved the way for later Volvo models and for firms like DAF and Scania to introduce chassis into Britain.

Volvo was also involved in another customer-driven exercise, in this case to produce a new double-deck underframe. The Scottish Bus Group, looking for a Bristol

Lodekka replacement, encouraged Volvo truck importers, Ailsa Trucks, to build a new front-engined model incorporating the 6.7-litre Volvo TD70 engine. This unit allowed a front entrance, rather in the style of the Guy Wulfrunian 14 years earlier, but the compact TD70 took up considerably less space than the Gardner 6LX and the result was a much more practical, and much more successful vehicle. Although SBG was to become a major Ailsa customer, the fact that it was a normal-height bus did cause some problems in a group that had standardised on lowheight buses. A lowheight Ailsa was built, for Derby, but was not regarded as a successful bus.

The Ailsa was soon officially 'adopted' by Volvo and went on to sell around 1,000 chassis.

With the National up and running and the threat posed to its double-deck range by the Ailsa and Metropolitan, Leyland designers turned their minds to the next generation of double-deckers. The solution seemed to be the B15 project, a very advanced integral bus that would be sold as a

complete vehicle. The first B15s had the troublesome 501 engine, but when B15 was launched in 1977 as the Titan the Gardner 6LXB was the standard engine with Leyland's TL11 as an option. Fewer than 1,200 Titans were built, mainly for London, although this reflects more on resistance to its complexity rather than any reliability problems.

The interest in lighter-weight single-deckers continued and Bedford and Ford dominated this market. Bedford replaced its front-engined VAM model with the mid-engined 33ft YRQ in 1970; this used Bedford's 466 engine, mounted vertically under the floor. The 36ft YRT version appeared in 1972. Ford's equivalents, the R192 and R226, were redesignated R1014 and R1114 in 1971; these had tubocharged front-mounted engines, inclined at an angle after 1977 to give a lower floor line.

Smaller buses were still very much a minority interest in the 1970s. Seddon's Midi had sold in limited numbers, and one of the most promising new designs failed because it may have been ahead of its time. Bedford's JJL of 1976 was a stylish 27-seat rear-engined midibus, but Bedford was looking for volume production and the British market was not yet ready for small buses.

In the 1980s, of course, that would all change. ♠

Opposite left: **Outside London, the biggest fleet of Leyland's new-generation Titan model was built up by Greater Manchester PTE, which took 15 in 1978-80. They had bodies built by Park Royal, and were part of an order for 50; like several Titan orders, the rest were cancelled.**
Gavin Booth

Below: **Two typical 1970s buses – a Bristol VRT with ECW body and a Leyland National. In fact the VRT was a 1980 delivery to Southdown, and behind it is a 1983 National 2 for Brighton Borough. They wear a special Shuttle livery carried for a period by buses on some new joint services.**
Gavin Booth

Bottom: **Rather different municipal buses were the Bedford SB5s with Willowbrook 41-seat bodies bought by Aberconwy Borough Council in 1976 for its difficult service to St Tudno's Church.**
Gavin Booth

A CHANGE of government in 1979 signalled yet another vast upheaval for the bus industry, and the dust is still settling. With Margaret Thatcher as prime minister, the Conservatives were moving towards a free market economy and were determined to do away with what they saw as inefficient and management-heavy nationalised industries.

The first signs came with the 1980 Transport Act which deregulated express coach services for the first time in half a century. It is probably fair to say that the outcome was successful, although not perhaps as envisaged. At the start there was the sudden rush of new entrants to the market, including the potentially powerful British Coachways consortium, but state-owned National Express went in fighting with new and improved services and competitive fares, and can be seen as the ultimate winner. Its Scottish counterpart, SBG's Scottish Citylink, was slower to start but built up a successful Scottish-based network that complemented National Express.

A feature of the 1980 Act was the setting up of Trial Areas in different parts of Britain where local bus services could be run without the need for Road Service Licences. These, it was argued, would test the government's theories on local bus service deregulation. Three Trial Areas were designated. Two were rural, in Devon and Norfolk, and, perhaps unsurprisingly, little happened. The third, around Hereford, found Midland Red West facing some tough competition on routes it had previously monopolised, often from operators that were long-established, with substantial local goodwill.

What happened was quite prophetic – a taste of what would happen throughout Britain after 1986 – free buses, racing for passengers, cut-price fares, a multitude of operators competing for a limited amount of traffic. Operators in other parts of Britain watched with interest and concern. Some smaller operators, and the more entrepreneurial big companies, saw unlimited opportunities if this principle was extended across the rest of the country, as seemed almost inevitable. The concerned companies were those who enjoyed the security of monopoly and subsidy, and possibly knew how vulnerable they could be to attack.

The Hereford experiment was judged a success, of course, and helped convince politicians that the deregulated recipe was right for Britain – outside London, of course. The argument that the larger companies were able to sustain a planned network of services by cross-subsidising marginal services from profitable ones was not accepted; indeed 'cross-subsidy' became a dirty word, even though parts of the bus industry were largely built on cross-subsidy – between routes, between peak and off-peak traffic. Sunday and evening services often survived because of cross-subsidy

Left: **The use of minibuses on high-frequency services in place of double-deckers started in the 1980s. This Brighton & Hove 20-seat Mercedes-Benz L608D converted by Alexander is seen in April 1986 climbing high above Brighton.**
Gavin Booth

Above: **When the Brighton & Hove company was split away from Southdown, it adopted this attractive new livery, seen on a 1980 Bristol VRT series 3 with ECW bodywork.**
Gavin Booth

Another new name to appear in the mid-1980s was Badgerline, the former country area of Bristol Omnibus, which used a green/yellow livery with an amusing badger motif. This 1980 Leyland National 2 52-seater is seen in Bath.
Gavin Booth

Bristol Omnibus adopted this bold livery for its City Clipper services in Bristol, worn here by a 1981 Roe-bodied Leyland Olympian.
Gavin Booth

Exeter was the birthplace of the minibus revolution and Ford Transit 160Ds with bodies converted at the Midland Red Carlyle Works were used by Devon General to replace less-frequent big buses. Different liveries were used for groups of routes.
Gavin Booth

and after deregulation would disappear substantially from the commercial networks offered.

Much management time in the early 1980s was focussed on express service deregulation, with NBC and SBG fighting to retain their prestige express services and build up new links while municipal, PTE and indep-endent fleets grasped the new opportunities. A new breed of upmarket coach, suited for high-speed, high-mileage services emerged, and the UK bodybuilders at last started to offer coach body styles that had the flair of the continentals.

Relaxed

It is sometimes forgotten that bus service licensing was relaxed sufficiently after 1980 to allow new operators to challenge the incumbents on profitable routes. Few took advantage of this freedom but there were two celebrated cases. Yeowarts started services in Whitehaven in 1981 in direct competition with NBC subsidiary, Cumberland, and there was much concern that one small operator could destabilise a network. And in Cardiff, CK Coaches started to compete with Cardiff City Transport using ex-London DMS-type Daimler Fleetlines.

All of these early skirmishes were a taste of what was to come.

The perceived success of the Trial Areas led the government to take things to their logical conclusion. The 1985 Transport Act brought far-reaching changes to the structure and operation of the bus industry. All local bus services outside London would be deregulated, with no need for licensing, and the National Bus Company would be privatised.

The stage was set for a major reorganisatiom of the state-owned sector of the bus industry in preparation for deregulation. In place of the larger operating units created in the 1970s following the merger of Tilling and BET under NBC, that organisation now found itself breaking down these units, sometimes to create more manageable companies, and sometimes to create companies whose operating areas were more closely related to county boundaries.

Old names reappeared – Brighton & Hove, Devon General, North Western, Provincial, South Midland, Southern National, Wilts & Dorset – and new names were introduced – including Cambus, Cheltenham & Gloucester, Hampshire Bus, Hastings & District, Northumbria. Changes were made to the previously sacrosanct NBC corporate livery styles, and some stylish new liveries appeared.

In Scotland SBG was preparing for deregulation by creating four new bus-operating companies in 1985. Lowland and Strathtay were hived off from larger companies to position managers closer to their local markets. The two most prominent of the new SBG companies were Clydeside and Kelvin, both based in the Glasgow area where SBG expected intensive competition from Strathclyde Buses. Both new companies adopted an aggressive marketing-led approach to deregulation, including the use of ex-London Routemasters on intensive urban services.

The competitive use of secondhand RMs had been started by Stagecoach, then still a small Perth-based express and local service operator, and several other companies would recognise the value of RMs as an inexpensive but effective tool for short-term competitive advantage.

A new municipal name was Inter Valley Link, the renamed Rhymney Valley undertaking. This long Leyland Olympian with East Lancs coach-seated bodywork is seen at the Leyland 90 celebrations in 1986.
Gavin Booth

Lowland Scottish was one of the new Scottish Bus Group companies created in 1985. A Seddon Pennine VII with Alexander Y-type bodywork is seen at Galashiels in the original light green/yellow livery, with SBG's 'Best Bus' vinyls on the side.
Stewart J Brown

During this period London Transport had its fair share of problems. The Greater London Council's 'Fares Fair' initiative cut fares in 1981 and increased bus and underground ridership, but was sabotaged by Bromley council who brought an action to rule it illegal. The GLC was not popular with government and although a fares cut was introduced in 1983 the GLC's future was under threat. In 1984 the Capital's transport planning passed to the new London Regional Transport, with the new London Buses Ltd as its bus-operating subsidiary, set up the following year.

Although the effects of the 1985 Act are outside the scope of this book, readers will be aware of the massive upheaval that followed. The spread of the minibus and a number of lean years for big bus manufacturers as Britain struggled through a recession; the break-up of NBC and the new groupings that have emerged from its ashes; the birth of a new breed of competitive and sometimes aggressive bus operator; the demise of once-famous companies; the rise of the midibus and the enthusiastic return of Dennis to the ranks of the bus builders; the increasing proportion of imported vehicles; the demise of Leyland into the Volvo fold; the privatisation of Scottish Bus Group and London Buses.

There were already hints of what was to come before the 1985 Act came into effect in October 1986 – in particular the return of the minibus. Not that it had ever really been away, but larger operators had tended to shy clear of running them because unions insisted on drivers being paid at big bus rates. The Devon General company was instrumental in negotiating minibus rates for drivers and introducing minibuses on frequent services in place of

Above: **The Routemaster, first introduced more than 20 years earlier, was still the mainstay of many central London routes well into the 1980s.** *Gavin Booth*

Right: **The West Midlands PTE Tracline experiment where a short length of guided busway was installed in suburban Birmingham, used MCW Metrobus MkIIs with special guidewheels to run in the concrete guideway.** *Gavin Booth*

Left: **To replace its RF type single-deckers London Transport went for Bristol LH6Ls in 1976/7 with ECW 39-seat bodies, and one is seen in Claygate in 1982.**
Geoff Rixon

Below: **London Transport bought two MkII MCW Metrobuses in 1985 as part of its vehicle evaluation programme. The MkII was a simpler version of the Metrobus using fewer parts.**
Gavin Booth

full-size buses. Several other NBC companies followed Devon General's example and the buses most regularly used were Ford Transit parcel vans converted to 16-seat buses – the archetypal 'breadvans'. The minibus as a vehicle was refined over the years and grew bigger, with many operators moving to 25-seaters and even 31-seaters, at which point a new type of midibus took over, a breed spearheaded by the Dennis Dart.

It is convenient to think of the minibus as a post-deregulation phenomenon; certainly the peak minibus sales occurred in the late 1980s but even in 1984-6 the numbers increased dramatically, admittedly from a low base.

An early taste of another later phenomenon was the introduction in 1984 of a short (600m) length of guided busway in suburban Birmingham, served by West Midlands PTE MCW Metrobuses fitted with special guidewheels. Although the Tracline system was fairly short-lived, more permanent guided busways have appeared in Britain, and many see this as an acceptably low-cost salternative to light rail.

The major upheavals of the 1980s, following closely on the changes of 1968/9, meant that the rules have been constantly changing over the past 30 years; by comparison the previous 20 years had been relatively uneventful. ♠

A RASH of new bus types was taking to the streets in the early 1980s, ironically just in time for an unexpected downturn in orders and a time of crisis for manufacturers.

The five top-selling double-deck buses in 1981, for instance, were the Leyland Atlantean (660 sales in Britain), the MCW Metrobus (649), the Bristol VRT (392), the Leyland Titan (135) and the Dennis Dominator (95). A year later the situation had changed significantly, reflecting the run-out of older models and increased orders for new types. Best-seller was the MCW Metrobus (406), followed by the Leyland Olympian (360), Leyland Atlantean (282), Leyland Titan (275) and Dennis Dominator (159).

The Metrobus continued to sell well until 1989 when the Laird Group decided to sell MCW. Leyland's 1980-introduced Olympian quickly established itself as market-leader and survived Leyland's purchase by Volvo to emerge as the Volvo Olympian. Like the Titan before it, but unlike previous generations of Leyland double-decker, the Olympian offered a choice of Leyland or Gardner engines, and when Leyland engines ceased to be made, the Cummins L10 engine was offered. The Olympian became

The Volvo Citybus was the first successful underfloor-engined double-decker. This is the 1982 prototype, badged as an Ailsa, in service with Strathclyde PTE. It carries an 86-seat Marshall body.
Gavin Booth

Leyland's all-purpose double-decker – production of the Fleetline had ceased by 1981; the VRT went in 1980; the Ailsa and the Titan in 1984.

London orders were important to the future viability of the bus manufacturing industry. After the unfortunate experiences with the AEC Merlin/Swift family and the DMS-type Fleetlines – both classes had been withdrawn prematurely – LT was stocking up with advanced-specification double-deckers. Leyland and MCW fought hard to win London orders and ultimately 1,125 Titans and 1,443 Metrobuses were supplied new to LT. London was far and away the most important Titan customer, and the end of London orders signalled the end of Titan production. MCW had a range of other customers for the Metrobus, notably West Midlands, but the lack of London orders was an important factor in the Laird Group's decision to close MCW's bus bodybuilding plant.

At various times LT had toyed with new advanced own-design double-deckers in the tradition of the RT and RM, but nothing would come of these. It also looked at alternative double-deck types in 1984/5 when it bought three Dennis Dominators, three Leyland Olympians, two MkII MCW Metrobuses, and three Volvo Ailsas, and these trials led to an order for 260 Olympians, the last big bus order LT would place.

Just as production of the older models was winding down, three new double-deck chassis appeared in the 1980s, the Scania BR112DH, the Dennis Falcon V and the Volvo Citybus.

The Scania had a British-style transverse rear engine, the 11-litre Scania DN11, and has continued in production as the N112 and N113. The Falcon V was essentially a single-deck chassis with a compact 10.96-litre Mercedes-Benz V6 engine under the floor at the rear – only six double-deckers were built.

The Volvo Citybus was a double-deck chassis based on the B10M underfloor-engined single-deck chassis, and became the first bus of this type to go into production. Leyland countered with the Lion, introduced in 1985 and built by its Danish subdsidiary, DAB, but sales were limited.

Sales of single-deck buses plummeted in the early 1980s. From a peak of around 1,000 in 1978, sales dropped to just 130 in 1982. The Leyland National was clear market-leader and with sales so low Leyland chose to stop production in 1985 and replace it with a new bus, also built at Workington, available as a complete bus or separate underframe. Production of the Lynx started in 1985.

Operators looking for underfloor-engined chassis from Leyland still had the Leopard but this was showing its age by 1980 when compared with imports from Volvo and DAF.

Above: **Most of the PTEs tried Volvo Ailsas, and while some built up sizeable fleets, Greater Manchester had just three, with 79-seat Northern Counties bodies, bought in 1980/2. This is one of the 1982 buses, wearing GM's brown/orange/white livery, in Wigan.**
Gavin Booth

Left: **The Lion was Leyland's answer to the Volvo Citybus, but it was never a serious rival. The first were delivered in 1986 to Eastern Scottish with Alexander 86-seat bodies.**
Gavin Booth

The Olympian has proved to be the most successful double-deck model of the 1980s and 1990s; this is the Leyland prototype, delivered in 1980 to Ribble with lowheight ECW bodywork – a combination that would quickly become familiar in many parts of Britain. It is seen when new on a rally; 'B45' in the route number box refers to the Leyland development number.
John Robinson

It was replaced by the Tiger, introduced in 1982, an improved chassis with air suspension and more powerful engines that was used mainly as a coach chassis, but was also favoured by several operators, notably Scottish Bus and Ulsterbus for bus work.

Other Leyland single-deck models still on the lists were the Bristol LH, to 1981, the midi-sized front-engined Cub, introduced in 1979, and the faithful Bristol RE, no longer available in Britain but built for 'export' customers Ulsterbus/Citybus until 1982.

More competition

Leyland was facing more competition than it did in the early 1970s. Volvo's B58 was replaced by the hugely successful B10M in 1980, and by the end of the decade had toppled the Leyland Tiger as best-selling coach chassis. Scania's N112 and subsequent N113 were also sold as single-deck buses. Seddon's Pennine VII remained in production until 1982.

There were two newcomers in the early 1980s. Quest 80 built chassis at Telford, usually for export, but some

rear-engined chassis were chosen by British operators for bus and coach use – though without much success. Ward Brothers built the Dalesman coach chassis in small numbers from 1980 and in 1983 built six Gardner rear-engined chassis, type GRXI, for Darlington Transport.

Dennis bounced back into the bus market in the early 1980s with a whole range of single-deck chassis. There was the Falcon, a full-size rear-engined bus with Gardner 6HLXB engine; the Falcon V, a single-deck coach; the lightweight Lancet with mid-mounted Perkins vertical engine; the Dorchester, a full-size Gardner mid-engined chassis; and the midi-size Domino with transverse rear-mounted Perkins engine. None of these types sold particularly well, but in the 1990s Dennis hit the big time with its Dart chassis.

The growth of the motorway system in Britain and the demand for high-powered up-market coaches – particularly following the deregulation of express services in 1980 – meant that onetime coach market leaders Bedford and Ford were suffering from dropping sales.

Bedford's mid-engined 11m YMT model was replaced by the turbocharged YNT and the 12m air-suspended Venturer YNV followed in 1984 and might have revived the company's fortunes had parent company General Motors not decided to close Bedford down two years later.

A year earlier Ford had stopped building full-size bus and coach chassis and concentrated on vans and trucks, and of course the majority of the early deregulation minibuses were based on Ford Transit parcel vans. The Mercedes-Benz L608D was chosen by some, though its narrow body was seen as a deterrent by several operators; only when Mercedes introduced more suitable minibus chassis did it move into first place among minibus builders for the UK market. The Dodge S50, later badged as a Renault, was another contender in the early days, along with the Iveco Daily.

The sales of new buses in 1980 – over 5,400 vehicles – were artificially high, partly because operators were rushing to register new buses before the Bus Grants were reduced from the 50% level. As deregulation and NBC privatisation approached, orders dropped dramatically, and as manufacturers struggled to make sensible use of resources, factory closures were inevitable. Before deregulation Leyland had closed Park Royal and Roe, ECW would follow soon afterwards and unlikely as it seemed even in those difficult times, Leyland itself would disappear before too long. ♠

Above: **The Olympian was also popular with municipal fleets. This 1985 Chester City Transport example carries Northern Counties bodywork.**
Gavin Booth

Below: **South Yorkshire PTE built up the largest fleet of Dennis Dominators, the majority with Alexander R-type bodywork like this 1983 bus seen in Sheffield.**
Gavin Booth

A prototype Scania BR112DH with East Lancs bodywork acting
as a demonstrator with Warrington Borough in 1981.
John Robinson

13 *The final countdown*
Summing up

A taste of the future – in the short-term anyway. A Midland Red (North) Ford Transit 190D with 16-seat Dormobile body conversion, at Shrewsbury early in 1986. Most fleets painted minibuses in different colours and chose catchy fleetnames, though 'MiniBUS' was not necessarily one of the most original.
John Robinson

THE LACK of a clear and consistent transport policy for Britain has meant that the bus industry has tended to be a bit of a political football. The belief that state control was an essential ingredient in transport planning meant that at one time, more than four of every seven buses and coaches in Britain were in public ownership – whether state- or local authority-owned.

In retrospect this had good points and bad points. With strict regulation of bus services the nationalised territorial companies were able to provide a good level of service as dominant operators in everything from busy cities like Bristol and Norwich to remote areas like North Wales and Caithness, with an internal system of cross-subsidy ensuring that uneconomic services survived, shored up by the urban and interurban networks. The state ownership of Bristol and ECW meant that Tilling, and to a lesser degree SBG, had access to well-proven, well-built buses to highly-standardised designs, which were economical to run. Of course there were the inefficiencies that result from monopoly – a sense of complacency, a lack of innovation, an unwillingess to respond to public pressures.

Although the BET group of companies, whose operating areas largely complemented the Tilling companies in

England and Wales, were privately owned, passengers living in areas served by their services enjoyed many of the same benefits.

Municipal bus services were often a matter of intense local pride, and Corporations invested heavily in new buses and in infrastructure such as garages, workshops and bus stations. The PTEs carried forward this tradition, capitalising on their vast buying power to develop new breeds of standard vehicle, and their ability to influence manufacturers. Some of the PTEs will also be remembered for their willingness to innovate and their pursuit of a truly integrated transport system.

The first and biggest 'PTE', London Transport, has always been very much in the spotlight. Everything it tried to do was in full glare of the Palace of Westminster, and while in its heyday LT was an undeniably impressive organisation, developing some of the classic buses of all time, it seemed

Above: **This prototype Leyland Lynx was built in 1985 and entered service with Ribble before deregulation, and is seen in the village of Withnell. The Lynx was launched on to the market when it was particularly depressed, and it took some time before sales started to pick up.**
Gavin Booth

Below: **Midland Fox, part of the split Midland Red company, chose a bold livery with a yellow diagonal at the front. This Fox Cub seen in Leicester in 1985 is a Ford Transit with 16-seat Rootes-converted body.**
Gavin Booth

Above and opposite top: **Two reminders that minibuses existed in big companies before the 1980s. London Country was using this Ford Transit (above) on dial-a-ride services in Harlow in 1975, and West Yorkshire used two of these Deansgate-bodied Ford Transits (opposite top) on a 'Chauffeur Coach' service in Harrogate in 1976.**
Gavin Booth

to lose its way in the 1960s and later became a pawn in the pitched battle between the government and the GLC.

And working away in the background have been the independent bus operators, some with a mere handful of buses, others with substantial fleets. Many were family firms and most had a long and proud tradition of bus operation. Over the years some of the most prominent firms succumbed to approaches made by the territorial companies and deregulation has signalled the end for many more who were not prepared to fight on under the new rules; but with entry into the bus market relatively easy and low-cost, there are new firms appearing all the time, and some have grown to a size and importance that few could have anticipated.

All of these factors have influenced bus design, along with such elements as legal dimensions and other legislation, the spread of driver-only operation, changes in passenger demand, and the state of the manufacturing industry.

As demand for new buses fluctuated, manufacturers have fallen by the wayside, all part of the natural process. Manufacturers had always tended to respond to operator demands for more seating capacity, more powerful engines, easier gearboxes, lighter weight – but in the 1960s and 1970s the officially-encouraged growth of the Leyland empire artificially affected the market by reducing choice and offering buses on a 'take-it-or-leave-it' basis. This in turn stimulated competition, most notably from mainland Europe, which brought changes that have had a lasting effect.

For many the disappearance of once-proud names is a matter of great regret. A quarter of a century ago it was inconceivable that manufacturers such as AEC, Bedford, Bristol, Daimler, Guy and Leyland would no longer be building bus chassis, and that Duple, ECW, MCW, Park Royal, Roe and Willowbrook would no longer be building bus bodies. Or that there would no longer be bus operators called Central SMT, Hants & Dorset, Southdown, Thames Valley or Western Welsh.

But it would be wrong to paint a rose-tinted picture of the bus industry in the 1950-86 period. It certainly had its problems, not least a failure to face up to the steady decline in passenger numbers and the complacency that comes with monopoly and public ownership.

Today's British bus industry is very different. There are aspects which those raised on the idea of transport as a public service may find difficult to accept, but there is little doubt that the need to act commercially has produced some leaner and fitter companies, and the move towards lower-floor, easier to use, environmentally cleaner buses was definitely overdue, and a far cry from the high-floor buses that often seemed to have been designed by engineers for ease of maintenance and traffic staff for maximum capacity,

Below: **Several British cities have suffered from wall-to-wall buses following deregulation. Glasgow bus services were deregulated before the official D-day, and there were immediately problems with the sheer volume of buses on some city streets. This September 1986 view shows yellow-fronted Kelvin and orange Strathclyde Buses vehicles.**
Gavin Booth

without any thought for the passenger or indeed the poor driver.

A belated acknowledgement that public transport could help solve many of our environmental and urban congestion problems means that the bus has an assured future, particularly as the cost of new tramway and light rail schemes has risen. Compared with today's bus industry, the years before deregulation seem to belong to a different world, but the developments between 1950 and 1986 played a very important part in the story of Britain's buses, and deserve to be remembered. ♠

Table I
Major UK bus fleets 1952

FLEET TOTALS

Municipals	20,844
London Transport	9,921
BET group	11,736
Tilling group	10,310
Scottish Bus Group	4,319

TEN LARGEST BRITISH FLEETS

London Transport	9,921
Glasgow Corporation	2,047
Birmingham City	1,919
Midland Red	1,803
Alexanders	1,768
Manchester Corporation	1,533
Crosville	1,287
Liverpool Corporation	1,117
Ribble	1,155
Bristol Tramways	1,150

Source: The Little Red Book 1952/3

Then-independent Lancashire United had over 400 buses in 1952, including this 1944 Guy Arab with utility Strachans 56-seat body. Like many operators, LUT's first Guys were utilities in 1942, and it went on to buy Guys until 1967.
A J Douglas/Photobus

Table 2
Major UK bus fleets 1968

MUNICIPALS AND THEIR FLEETS

Aberdare 36, Aberdeen 239, Accrington 55, Ashton-under-Lyne 60, Barrow 64, Bedwas & Machen 7, Belfast‡ 517, Birkenhead 227, Birmingham 1545, Blackburn 104, Blackpool§ 294, Bolton 255, Bournemouth‡ 161, Bradford‡ 429, Brighton 62, Burnley Colne & Nelson 147, Burton 47, Bury 96, Caerphilly 33, Cardiff‡ 255, Chester 50, Chesterfield 137, Colchester 43, Colwyn Bay 5, Coventry 308, Darlington 65, Darwen 32, Derby‡ 162, Doncaster 109, Douglas 45, Dundee 242, Eastbourne 55, Edinburgh 707, Exeter 66, Gelligaer 30, Glasgow 1244, Great Yarmouth 65, Grimsby & Cleethorpes 104, Halifax 179, Hartlepool 71, Haslingden 15, Huddersfield‡ 205, Hull 238, Ipswich 68, Lancaster 37, Leeds 673, Leicester 204, Leigh 59, Lincoln 60, Liverpool 1200, Llandudno 10, Lowestoft 15, Luton 68, Lytham St Annes 37, Maidstone 45, Manchester 1297, Merthyr Tydfil 72, Middlesbrough 100, Morecambe & Heysham 47, Newcastle 350, Newport 99, Northampton 88, Nottingham 391, Oldham 211, Plymouth 240, Pontypridd 56, Portsmouth 183, Preston 96, Ramsbottom 12, Rawtenstall 45, Reading‡ 111, Rochdale 135, Rotherham 136, St Helens 142, Salford 276, Sheffield 773, South Shields 87, Southampton 189, Southend 82, Southport 60, SHMD 91, Stockport 162, Stockton 103, Sunderland 193, Swindon 71, Teesside 42, Todmorden 34, Wallasey 75, Walsall 277, Warrington 71, West Bridgford 28, West Bromwich 129, West Mon 30, Widnes 40, Wigan 151, Wolverhampton 304.

§Fleet also running trams. ‡ Fleets also running trolleybuses.

LONDON TRANSPORT

8219 (buses)

TILLING GROUP COMPANIES AND THEIR FLEETS

Bath 148, Brighton Hove & District 149, Bristol 1058, Charlie's Cars 12, Cheltenham District 34, Crosville 1140, Cumberland 192, Durham District 70, Eastern Counties 750, Eastern National 656, Hants & Dorset 478, Keighley-West Yorkshire 52, Lincolnshire 386, Mansfield District 113, Midland General 197, Notts & Derby 37, Red & White 395, Shamrock & Rambler 30, Southern National 377, Southern Vectis 182, Thames Valley 361, Tilling 24, United Auto 1042, United Counties 476, United Welsh 161, West Yorkshire 424, Western National 606, Wilts & Dorset 275, York-West Yorkshire 74.

SCOTTISH BUS GROUP COMPANIES AND THEIR FLEETS

Alexanders (Fife) 519, Alexanders (Midland) 995, Alexanders (Northern) 597, Central SMT 650, Highland Omnibuses 189, Scottish Omnibuses 900, Western SMT 1051.

BET GROUP COMPANIES AND THEIR FLEETS

Aldershot & District 285, Altrincham Coachways 8, BMMO 1780, Black & White 114, County 23, Devon General 278, East Kent 610, East Midland 224, East Yorkshire 246, Gateshead & District 68, Greenslades 80, Hebble 73, Maidstone & District 772, Melba Motors 10, Mexborough & Swinton 50, Neath & Cardiff 31, North Western 553, Northern General 624, City of Oxford 223, Potteries 506, Red Line 6, Rhondda 164, Ribble 1093, Samuelson 18, Scout 47, Sheffield United Tours 103, Southdown 897, South Wales 333, Standerwick 82, Stratford Blue 44, Sunderland District 95, Thomas Bros 53, Timpson 99, Trent 380, Tynemouth 73, Tyneside 17, Wakefields 15, Western Welsh 570, Yorkshire Traction 339, Yorkshire Woollen 268.

ULSTERBUS

1170

SIGNIFICANT PRIVATE COMPANIES AND THEIR FLEETS

West Riding 406, Lancashire United 391, Barton 347, Wallace Arnold 307, David MacBrayne 137.

FLEET TOTALS

Municipals	17,777
London Transport	8,219
BET group	11,000
Tilling group	9,899
Scottish Bus Group	4,901

TEN LARGEST BRITISH FLEETS

London Transport	8,219
Midland Red	1,780
Birmingham City	1,545
Manchester Corporation	1,297
Glasgow Corporation	1,244
Liverpool Corporation	1,200
Crosville	1,140
Ribble	1,093
Bristol Omnibus	1,058
Western SMT	1,051

Source: The Little Red Book 1968

New to United Auto in 1968, when the company still had more than 1,000 buses and coaches, a Bristol LH6L with 45-seat ECW body, one of the first of a fleet of over 200 LHs for lighter duties. It is seen picking up passengers at Goathland in 1976.
Gavin Booth

Table 3
Major UK bus fleets 1985

MUNICIPALS AND THEIR FLEETS

Aberconwy§ 10, Barrow 47, Blackburn 91, Blackpool§ 184, Bournemouth 144, Brighton 54, Burnley & Pendle 96, Cardiff 197, Chester 50, Chesterfield 118, Cleveland 215, Colchester 54, Colwyn 2, Cynon Valley 30, Darlington 56, Derby 132, Eastbourne 46, East Staffs 38, Fylde 32, Grampian 199, Great Yarmouth 50, Grimsby & Cleethorpes 71, Halton 34, Hartlepool 71, Hyndburn 47, Ipswich 73, Islwyn 30, Hull 245, Lancaster 51, Leicester 251, Lincoln 40, Lothian 583, Maidstone 41, Merthyr Tydfil 61, Newport 94, Northampton 67, Nottingham 354, Plymouth 163, Portsmouth 116, Preston 82, Reading 142, Rhymney Valley 69, Rossendale 50, Southampton 146, Southend 119, Taff-Ely 26, Tayside 180, Thamesdown 95, Warrington 65.

§Fleet also running trams.

LONDON TRANSPORT

5132

NATIONAL BUS COMPANY SUBSIDIARIES AND THEIR FLEETS

Alder Valley 388, Ambassador 84, Bristol 535, Cambus 172, Cheltenham & Gloucester 183, Crosville 933, Cumberland 148, Devon General 307, Eastern Counties 257, Eastern National 426, East Kent 316, East Midland 243, East Yorkshire 165, Hampshire Bus 185, Hastings & District 72, Lincolnshire 187, London Country 1134, Maidstone & District 348, Midland Fox 210, Midland Red Express 62, Midland Red North 258, Midland Red South 165, Midland Red West 203, National Travel East 152, National (London) 46, National Welsh 404, North Devon 59, Northern General 683, City of Oxford 134, Pilgrim 23, Potteries 254, Provincial 78, Ribble 872, Shamrock & Rambler 37, Southdown 542, Southern National 158, Southern Vectis 137, South Midland 84, South Wales 308, Trent 380, United Auto 741, United Counties 514, Wessex National 42, Western National 257, West Riding 282, West Yorkshire 345, Wilts & Dorset 210, Yorkshire Traction 329, Yorkshire Woollen 87, York-West Yorkshire 63.

SCOTTISH BUS GROUP COMPANIES AND THEIR FLEETS (1986 FIGURES)

Central 498, Clydeside 385, Eastern 406, Fife 305, Highland 217, Kelvin 444, Lowland 111, Midland 285, Northern 252, Strathtay 144, Western 327.

ULSTERBUS

1000

SIGNIFICANT PRIVATE COMPANIES AND THEIR FLEETS

Barton 240, Wallace Arnold 190, Shearings 110, Smith Happiways 105, Guernseybus 89, Isle of Man Transport 80, A1 Service 76, Grey-Green 72, OK 69.

FLEET TOTALS

Municipals	5,134
PTEs	9,423
London Transport	5,132
National Bus	14,202
Scottish Bus Group	4,257

TEN LARGEST BRITISH FLEETS

London Transport	5,132
London Country	1,134
Crosville	933
Ribble	872
United Auto	741
Northern General	683
Lothian Region Transport	583
Southdown	542
Bristol Omnibus	535
United Counties	514

Source: The Little Red Book 1968
          (SBG figures from 1987 edition)

The shape of 1985 buses – a Western National Mercedes-Benz L608D with Reeve Burgess 20-seat body, wearing Plymouth Hoppa fleetnames.
Gavin Booth